Diary of a Lover of Marilyn Monroe

Hans Jørgen Lembourn

Diary of a Lover of Marilyn Monroe

Translated by
Hallberg Hallmundsson

ARBOR HOUSE New York

To Ellen, my beloved

Diary of a Lover of Marilyn Monroe

1st Day

The voice. What I first met was the voice. And what I first thought was: This is not really her voice, here and now, in her East Side, New York, apartment on a half-dark afternoon. It must be a record someone is playing, a sound track from one of her films. It was the voice everyone knew, the one that sang about diamonds and "Bye, Bye Baby" and "Somebody Loves Me," the little-blonde-girl voice. There was never one like it before, and there probably never will be again, but everybody knows it and recognizes it, for hearing it you remember your most sex-conscious adolescent situations—what you thought were erotic confrontations with love but later turned into those moments of remembered affection that are tragic (in one's youth) and amusing (afterward). She can't talk that way off the screen, I thought. Her voice must be a professional trick; it can't be genuine.

But it was.

It whispered itself toward me from wherever she

I

was, through the rooms and into the room where I was sitting, waiting for her. I could hear fragments of what she was saying; it wasn't a record or tape. It was her, on the telephone, somewhere in the eerie half-empty apartment where all the doors stood open —eerie because there was at least one person there with her, and perhaps more, though none could be seen. There was also the apparently busy lady who had answered the door and quickly ushered me through an entrance hall with—as I remember— white, slender furniture, through a living room with white walls, a white piano, white sofa, white rugs, and a vase with white, artificial flowers, and into this room. There were marks on the walls where pictures had been removed, a few chairs, and a desk, all without style or coherence, either about to be taken away or the beginnings of something entirely new. Leaning against one wall was a portrait of Abraham Lincoln, taken down or about to be hung, and on the wall behind the desk there was a photo of her, dressed in a white robe. In a delicate, unprovocative way, the model and the photographer together had managed to communicate to the viewer that she was not wearing anything beneath the white terry cloth.

"Yes, it's $100,000 plus ten percent. Fred says it's all right, but I'm afraid of it, anyway . . . No, I haven't discussed it with *him*, he's not interested, anyway; he doesn't understand, you know he doesn't. It was never any good; he just sits and squints at me and says yes and no, and while he says it, I'm thinking he's just saying what I want most to hear, or else he says nothing at all and asks if there's spaghetti in the house. (Silence, listening.) No, *he*'s not here and hasn't been here . . . Still believes in it? Yeah, maybe, but I don't; it's over . . . No, well—yes—it's a mess, I haven't got the strength to clear it up, and there's nobody to help me, and they wouldn't even if I asked them . . . *I* have won out over them! That was yesterday. They're back today, and they're more of them and bigger and stronger, and you can keep winning out over them, and they always come back; didn't somebody once say something about losing every battle except the last one? . . . Yeah, them, they didn't like me either . . ."

The voice rose and fell, from a sort of cooing to whispering and back again, and then it became inaudible; she must have turned or pulled the door closed. But the sound still came through, this sound of honey, a call, directed only at you because it held out promises that no one else could hear. From time to time intelligible sentences could be heard, the conversation repeating itself around the same subject, always back to where it began, but still continuing—a desperate circle she wanted to, but could not, break out of . . .

It grew darker outside, ghost time creeping in from the Atlantic over the city's neon-light galaxy, and I continued waiting in the chair facing the desk, where Fred, the agent who had introduced me to her and helped me draft my idea for a film and with whom I was now on first-name terms, had planted himself in the desk chair beneath her picture.

We had been through the whole politeness routine and all the possible small talk, and we had no taste for more, and we didn't want to talk about the film either. We were afraid of talking the idea to death; so we waited.

Fred put out his fifth or sixth cigar, crushing the wet, chewed stub in the large, Mexican-looking ashtray, and looked at his watch.

"Only two hours, that's nothing! It may take three or four or five. As far as I know, her record is six hours, for shooting in a fully equipped studio with all systems ready! One film director said she makes woman-haters out of all of us."

Fred pulled a creased handkerchief out of the expansive folds of his unpressed suit—he was two hundred pounds or more—and wiped the perspiration from his forehead. That he had seated himself in the smallest chair in the room was clearly agent psychology; the armrests were pressing uncomfortably into his midriff bulge.

"You think we should go?"

"No, for God's sake, she'd be furious! There's no reason to ruin the whole project the very first day, is there? You have to be logical with her. Otherwise, it'll never go. She can't stand cigar smoke. At least, that's what she says."

He pulled a wastebasket from under the desk and spat a few pieces of cigar into it, extricated himself from his iron corset, took the ashtray, went over to the open window and looked down into the alley, emptied it, and returned to the center of the room. He waved his arms like a windmill in order to get the smell out, mopped himself with his handkerchief, panted asthmatically, closed the window, and sat down again in the confining chair, pushing himself into it sideways, first under one armrest, then, umpphh, under the other, getting both of them over his bulge again.

"Logical?"

"Yes, I'm very logical; that's why I'm such a good agent. Your project, by the way, is excellent."

Fred took out his cigar case but stopped, looked tenderly at the contents, swore, and put it back into his jacket.

"I'm glad to hear that. Anyway, I don't mind waiting."

"Good, good, you'll need all your patience, more than you can imagine."

"It can't be all that bad."

"Oo-la-la! There's a lot you don't know and will surprise you—that is, if we even get her to listen. You don't know her, but if you ever do, God help you, you'll need a lot of help."

"I let the sun go its way."

"Excuse me?"

"Oh, nothing."

"Will you put money into it?"

"My fee."

"That's not enough. If you believe in it yourself, you can make a lot of money on it."

"My fee, Fred."

"Tough, aren't you? After Irishmen and conceited playwrights, Scandinavians are the worst I know. But you're an exception."

"Thanks for that. What's wrong with Scandinavians?"

"They're so damn passive. They're all like celery. I can't stand celery. It bloats your stomach, makes you feel fatter than you actually are."

The voice came back; she must have turned or opened the door again. The sentences were the same, but the tone had changed ever so slightly, acquired a touch of desperation behind its sensuousness. I listened, and it changed again, became spirited, cheerful. Yet there was also an echo of sadness, there was anxiety and isolation and a groping for understanding. (There's a lot you don't know and that will surprise you!) This voice I had heard so often and now heard for the first time, coming from a room behind a room in a solitary apartment in a city bursting with people and running over with loneliness . . .

5

"You mustn't misunderstand me, I'm her friend," Fred was saying. "But she's very complex. Very complex."

Fred became lost in thought and kept turning the ashtray around and around and looking out of the window. I began to wonder how I would answer if I were asked for a one-sentence description of her voice: "It's a voice that's always trying to tell you a secret but never gets around to it." No, too arty. "It's a voice that says, 'Come try and kiss me, and see if you can pull it off!'" Even worse; too much of a movie. "It's the touch of a sound." Says nothing. It's an impossible task . . .

"Are you falling asleep?" asked Fred. "Shall I see if there's anything to drink in the house?"

"No, thanks, I was listening to her voice."

"Her voice? Oh yes, her voice. Everybody thought it was absolutely ludicrous, no grown-up person could talk like that without being crazy or permanently arrested in adolescence. But she sure made them listen."

All of a sudden she spoke out loud, evidently to someone in the apartment, and shortly afterward the lady who had shown me in entered the room.

"I'm to bring you regards and ask your apology, but Miss Monroe can't manage to see you today. Can you come back tomorrow or the day after? I'll let Fred know."

"Tomorrow and tomorrow and the day after," said Fred, getting up. "We'll be back tomorrow. Or the day after. We'll always be back tomorrow. Or the day after. Bye-bye and best regards."

As the elevator door was closing, Fred pulled out his cigar, lit it, and puffed until his face disappeared in smoke. From inside the gray-blue cloud I heard him say in a harsh voice:

"It won't sound exactly charming to you, saying it

like this, but you'd better know how it is: Some people end up hating her, but most of them love her from the second they meet her and keep on loving her in spite of everything they can't stand because she needs protection. So I'm warning you, Mr. Up-and-Coming Screenwriter! I already warned myself, but it didn't help.

On his way through the lobby Fred saluted with two fingers touching the cap he wasn't wearing, and when we were out on the sidewalk he asked if he could give me a lift.

"No thanks, I'd rather walk."

"All the way uptown? You're a stubborn devil, aren't you?"

"And I think you're a shrewd psychologist, Fred."

"Ha, that's a good one! See you later!"

East Side, Manhattan, New York. The darkness was already blowing scraps of paper along the street.

2nd Day

Next day I sat in my hotel room, waiting. It was for nothing; no message came. I took out the proposal my publisher had sent to Fred; that's what had established the connection between us. Polished a few sentences. But it didn't come to much. My waiting was too intense.

I remember myself as I was—"the up-and-coming screenwriter"!—even though so many years have passed. I remember the impatient, nervous anticipation of waiting to meet a star. It was all so different from what I had imagined. There was no glamor. Good God, I was young and immature and uncertain—or rather, I was sure enough of myself but in an immature way. My remembrance of myself is melancholy (Melancholy Dane, I parody myself). I knew nothing of the tragedy, the wildness, and the sweetness too, that would take over. But I learned from it. I learned something about a woman's mind from a woman who could reach far beyond me in so many respects. It began in the great shadow the skyscrapers cast over the street and the apartment in which

I had waited, and which was about to be cast over a short life that would end in the most glaring sunlight I had ever experienced. Now the time has come when I feel I can—and must—tell about it. A hopeless love song may become the strongest incentive in a person's life. The love song within Marilyn was not without hope, but it was never completed.

3rd Day

There was no message that day either. But I would wait still another day before I called Fred. I was only a small chip in a big game played by others, and I didn't want to make myself ridiculous by pressing for something in which I was perhaps the only one to see anything important.

Instead, I went over to the West Side and took the sightseeing boat around Manhattan and out into New York Harbor, past the Statue of Liberty. I looked back at the city. In the bright light the skyscrapers stood out like columns of silver, all of different height, as if a temple were under construction in which all the columns would eventually be the same height and together form the Parthenon of the New World. It was in this temple that I would fight for my work. And in some nameless room in one of the columns a woman was sitting who, much to my surprise, appeared to be lonely. A vestal virgin watching over the fire I wouldn't dare approach? A friend who recognized my struggle as her own and wanted to share her victory with me? A bird that would fly away before I reached it, if someone whistled for it?

"Young man, you're stepping on my bag!" said an old woman, trying to pull her shopping bag away from me. She had leaned it up against the bulwark, and I had inadvertently put my foot on it.

"I'm sorry. I'm terribly, terribly sorry," I said, taking a quick step back.

"Well," she said. "It's not that terrible!"

4th Day

The message had come. Two hours early I was on my way down Broadway, taking an appropriately long detour to East Fifty-seventh Street, where her apartment was. The wind had died down, the sun was shining, and it was warm in the agreeable way it seldom is in New York. I was cheerful, in good form, excited, then felt a sudden flash of apprehension, and immediately afterward I began to steel myself for disappointment, if it should come. It was certain to. I would never capture the interest of such a famous star; I was too insignificant, too unknown. It was a wild idea I had dreamed up, something I alone could believe in—and then what? I was young, I had time, plenty of time; there were no firm plans, no promised dates. It was an experiment—one in which I was merely an incidental possibility that might be picked up but most likely would be passed over and never again remembered. Anything was possible.

Fred had told me: Stop talking about doing it; do it.

You can do anything if you only *do* it.

I went into a luncheonette and had a hamburger. If there was one door that wouldn't open, there were others that could be tried. I continued down Broadway through Manhattan's rectangular blocks to Times Square, where the newspaper tower rose like the sharp prow of a ship over waves of yellow taxis, red buses and colorful cars. There stood the little statue of Father Duffy, his hands folded, standing in front of a cross, peacefully listening to the syrupy hymn of "I'm in the Mood for Love." Then I turned back up Fifth Avenue between the poster signs for the Warners Cinerama Theatre and the castlelike department stores with their fur coats and diamonds. I consoled myself: I'm going west by going east; what will be, will be. I shook my head, a philosopher before my time.

I took other detours and reached the building on Fifty-seventh Street precisely at the prearranged time. Fred wasn't there. I asked the doorman if he had come and gone up, but he hadn't. In this business, it was clearly the norm to be late. But I couldn't expect her to condone my coming late, so I told the doorman I would go up now if he would announce me.

I rang the bell, and the same lady as before opened the door. This time I paid attention to her. She was very pale, and her features were sharp and sad; I felt as if I had entered a funeral parlor. I had the distinct feeling that she would prefer to be rid of me, that I was intruding and should not have been let in. She led me through the white entrance hall and the white living room. Two painters were fixing up a wall. On a bookshelf at the other end of the room stood three pictures of Marilyn, mounted—as far as I could see, rushing by—in a triptych sort of leather frame. There were inscriptions on the pictures, and each one showed her as the world saw

13

her—sexy, concealing yet revealing a nakedness that was inviting and lovely, with a smile just on the verge of laughter; the dream of every male. We came into the same room as before, which now had been furnished further: a sofa, shelves with books that had not been arranged, a vase with artificial flowers, white like those in the living room, and a few blue glasses. The last rays of the afternoon sun shone through the glasses so they came to dominate the unfinished room; it looked more blue than white.

"Miss Monroe will be with you in a moment," she said and left, so self-effacing that I didn't even hear her footsteps. I sat down in the same chair as yesterday, and waited. For a moment I wondered what I would say but gave up on it. Someone was knocking inside me.

Then she stood in the doorway.

She was wearing a white robe. She was small, smaller than I had expected; and heavier. Her face was smeared with glistening Vaseline. Her lips, slightly parted, had been given a touch of red. It was the only makeup she was wearing. She had tied a towel around her hair so snugly that not even the tiniest stray lock could be seen. She was barefoot. What I noticed most were her eyes, the lightest blue I had ever seen; like Delft tiles. No, tiles are inanimate, but behind the detectivelike observation of her eyes there was movement all the time. They were like swimming pools seen from aloft in a helicopter. Whether she just looked at me or blinked once or twice I can't remember; I disappeared into those eyes. They could be jumped down into—they invited it—but they would take notice of everything I did without reflecting the discoveries they made. I felt we stood there, face to face, for a long time, but of course it wasn't long at all.

She came over to me, warm and outgoing, smiled

cheerfully, held out her hand and bid me welcome, then turned around and went over to the sofa. There was a hint of that famous swing of her hips but not nearly as much as in her films. She sat down in the corner of the sofa with her feet drawn up under her, apparently oblivious of the fact that the robe slid open, baring her knee.

"It was nice of you to come again. I'm very sorry about the other time. I had to go somewhere and was already late. But you don't look like you mind very much."

"Not the least bit. I've got time enough."

"Time enough. It seems like ages since I've met anybody who had time enough, and I never have time enough myself, though . . . lately, things have begun to stand still. But I'm probably just in the midst of a pause. I've read your synopsis, and I agree with Fred—he's late—it's funny. I can see the idea: all the things a European may discover about us that we don't see because we're in the middle of it. I would like to play that part, even though—no, it leads too far, but we must talk about it. I'm committed to two more films, and then it's TV, which I would like to try; we have a fine idea. And Lee Strasberg, my teacher—do you know him?—he's sure that I'm now ready for the theater. I've always wanted that myself, and they all say I'm ready, and I believe it, but then, when I'm alone, I have second thoughts, and I have no one to . . . Hey, this sounds like a confession. I *did* have a father confessor once, but it didn't help either. Now, let's not talk about me all the time. What do you think of America?"

I told her what a shock it is to come face to face with America—it wasn't the first time I'd been there, but I hadn't forgotten the shock—the contrasts, the many frustrations, the poor, who still haven't realized their own situation and their opportunities, and then the success everybody thinks can be his because it looks so easy. I told her I had never known a society that had so many opportunities to transform itself, but in the midst of all the movement it apparently never quite did. It seemed to me as if it kept turning centrifugally around something that just wouldn't budge.

She bent forward, looked at me intensely, about to say something, but changed her mind, turned her head, and glanced out the window, suddenly looking as if she were in a trance and had left the room and the situation. I didn't understand what had happened. Had I said something to offend her or to remind her of something she was grieving over? For a few seconds she looked dead tired, her eyes glazed, her whole figure sagging a little. Then she put her arms around herself, pressing them up against her breasts, which in turn were pushed a bit upward. In her moment of surrender to fatigue I discovered that her nose was really a bit lumpy; I had never noticed that in her films. Then, thrusting her arms still further up and drawing her legs a bit tighter in under her, she was back with a big smile, and her eyes were very large. Even though she didn't move, her searching look made it appear that she leaned forward to give her words more weight; her eyes substituted for her body's movements.

"You say it's a shock. Don't you think it is for us, too? Do you know anything about my childhood? No! You would understand better if you did. I'm an orphan. I was shunted from one foster home to another and ended up in an orphanage. I had to teach myself everything I've ever learned; there was no one to help. You don't know how hungry I've been. And when I finally got to play a bit part in a film, it was cut out. You have no idea how hard it is. There isn't a single movement, not a single inflection in a line that I haven't learned by myself, working it over a thousand times. And I know films. I know them through and through, though people don't believe it; they think it's been a cinch to me. Even though there's been publicity about my orphaned childhood, it's never sunk in; people think it's something they make up. It isn't; it's true, every word of it. My mother . . . No, look, now we're talking about me again. You're from Denmark. Tell me something about Denmark!"

I nodded and told her something about Denmark—the location, the population, the climate, the welfare state. It didn't sound very exciting, but she listened as if it meant a great deal to her to learn and understand and gain knowledge.

"In that country I wouldn't have had such an unhappy childhood; it would all have been nicer," she said.

"To begin with, maybe, but not later," I said. "When all's said and done, I guess it all depends on you."

"Is that true? I'm not quite sure about that. But maybe you're right. I haven't been in Europe, only in England, and that was no success. Nobody taught me anything. I felt isolated; I wouldn't have been in Denmark. I think I would have been glad to be there. I can hear it in what you say. My father was a Norwegian, did you know that? I was born Mortensen! That's Danish, too, isn't it?"

"It's very Danish."

"There you see, it's probably there I really belong. Some say he was born in Denmark, my father, but I've never seen him. And never will either. He ran away from my mother on a motorcycle, which he was absolutely wild about, and was killed on a highway before I was born."

"Marilyn Monroe Miller Mortensen! You have a

fondness for the letter *M?*"

"*M?*"

She looked at me in wonderment, her eyes becoming still larger, and suddenly she laughed a short little squeaky laughter that made me think of a mouse (I later discovered that some of her stepparents had called her Mouse as an endearment). It was a girlish titter which should have served just to begin the laughter, but it never became anything more in terms of sound; instead, it sprang from her mouth to her eyes, which radiated gales of laughter.

"*M!*"

She dropped her defensive pose—the arms wrapped tightly around her body—and stretched them out; her robe opened a bit more, and she looked like the picture on the wall facing me. She was here and now, filling the whole room with her loveliness, and my heart was pounding so damn hard she must have heard it.

"*MMMMMMMM!* Yes, I like *M* very much; I never thought about that. How did you know? It's in the middle of the alphabet, isn't it? If the letters were building blocks and they were pushed together from both ends so they were piled up in a pyramid, *M* would be right on top!"

She pushed them together in the air, and there they stood, the *M* shining like a neon light over a Hollywood studio.

"Why haven't I ever noticed that before? *M* is a very important letter. Anything that has any meaning begins with an *M*—meet, mingle, marry, money, men—oh, this is delightful . . . But listen, I haven't asked you what you want to drink. You're from Denmark, do you like beer? Oh, but how can you? It's dreadful, so you won't get that. A Scotch? Straight or . . . ? With soda, good, coming right up."

I looked at her bare feet as she ran out of the room. I heard her clatter with glasses and bottles, and then she put on a record, and Frank Sinatra's eggnog voice floated through the apartment. She returned with glasses for both of us and a bottle of champagne under her arm and sat down again in the corner of the sofa in the same position as before. It was as if we had known each other for years and there was a conspiracy in the making. She bent around the sofa and pulled a low table to the front, let the champagne bottle pop, poured, toasted, and drank—bottoms up—then poured again.

"How about numbers? Do you like numbers like you do letters?"

"I didn't really say I liked letters—not that way—but, well, *M* is fine with me, too. Numbers?"

She looked at me, and I got sucked into those eyes.

"I like five the best," I said, "and all figures divisible by five, especially fifteen."

"Five? I'm fondest of one. What about colors?"

"Blue!"

"Truly?"

She clapped her hands.

"Blue and white; they're my colors, too. From now on I'll call you Hans, and you'll say Marilyn. It's as if we had known each other for a long time, isn't it?"

Her glass was empty and was refilled.

"So where does Monroe come from?" I asked.

"My grandfather's name was Otis Elmer Monroe, and my mother was born Gladys Pearl Monroe. A very good friend of mine found out that my mother's family can be traced back to America's fifth president, James Monroe, but the car has picked up a lot of dirt since then on the way through the generations. It's a successful family I belong to in America. Someone once said

I got interested in other nationalities because I was so parochially American, so I guess I can't be Norwegian or Danish. I'm not quite sure I understand what he meant by it, and yet . . . But you can explain that to me someday, you understand it; I'm sure you understand it. I have to have someone explain what it is I understand before I understand it! Are you thinking now it's because she's a dumb blonde, the way they usually say?"

"One doesn't get this far without having some kind of brains."

"Some kind? There are different kinds of brains— is that what you mean? I've met people who had lots of brains. They did all they could for me—they still would—but maybe they had a totally different kind of brains, brains that would not work for me? Is that possible?"

"Yes, that's possible."

"There'll be some sentences, some answers, and I feel they're the right ones, but then it stops. Suddenly there's jealousy or anger or secrets, something that shouldn't have been said and that hurts so much that love turns into hate and accusations, and then it's over, and the rest is play-acting for the sake of being sociable, exit the brains, and I'm just as lonely as before. I thought I was in for such excitement . . . No, it didn't work out this time either; it never does . . . But what am I doing? How would you understand all that? I'm no good at explaining, anyway. What's happening?"

"I'm just sitting quietly and listening. That's all."

She became silent—visibly so—her tongue running over her lower lip, and then she put her little finger and her ring finger half into her mouth and looked at me as if she had never seen me before. She wanted something, I didn't know what. The room had become half dark, and there was complete silence; no sound could be heard from the street, far down below. Her white robe, her glistening face, and her eyes shone. It was as if a skin of shiny material had been pulled over her own skin, so that she was more naked than naked, as if this were not New York but we were wandering, frightened, into a deserted territory and wanted to take each other's hand but didn't dare . . . And then Fred was in the doorway, filling it up completely. He was perspiring, and he mopped his forehead and muttered some unintelligible curse words. She jumped up, ran to him, put her arms around his neck, and almost shouted: "Ah, Fred, you're late! Listen, how dare you? Isn't it marvelous? Fred is late! Aren't you ashamed?"

He submitted to her embraces and then went with heavy steps over to the narrow chair and crammed himself into it.

"Traffic jam on Forty-fifth. Those idiots! What in hell do we pay taxes for? To have the police get rid of those nitwits who don't know the difference between left and right. And then they plant themselves right in front of you and play important. This poor sick town will stop functioning soon because the idiots don't know how to drive a car anymore; they think they have a general admissions ticket to an amusement park as soon as they get here! If you can write anything funny about driving a car in New York, then you're funnier than I think! Damn!"

She went and returned with a champagne glass and poured for him, and he gulped it down and looked at us irritably and yet as if he would grin if somebody could make him.

"Well, Fred, now we both know someone who likes to be late," she said.

"All right, Snotty," he said and poured himself another glass so the champagne ran over. "Have you gotten any work done?"

"No," she said.

"So what the hell have you been doing all this time?"

"Waiting," she said, smiling. "We couldn't do anything about it without you. Oh, it's a lovely day. And now it's too late. I should have been somewhere else half an hour ago, and I'm far from ready. I'll say it was your fault."

"Bah! I've got a draft of a contract with me."

"Put it away. Not now. It's too late. I don't have the time to talk movies now—and I don't want to either."

"Now, that's not funny. Listen here . . ."

"We've got plenty of time. I've just met Hans here, and he's got plenty of time, and it's your fault if we can't make it."

"Cut it out. Not everything in this goddam world is my fault."

"Yes, it is, Big Fatty, that's what you're paid for. It's nice to have someone who always takes all the blame."

Fred twisted himself out of the chair, panting.

"I'm not much of a churchgoer," he said, bouncing out of the room. He turned in the door, dried his wet face with his handkerchief, and said:

"So when you two have become a little less holy, we'll talk again."

He disappeared, and she laughed—not the mouse laughter, although the squeaky giggle was still there. But a warm, open laughter drowned it out, and she wiped her eyes on the sleeve of her robe.

"Fred is very sweet," she said. "He always comes around again. But really, I have to hurry. I'm sorry; I would have liked to sit here all evening."

We stood up, and she went ahead through the living room, past the secretary who—I noticed—looked at me

angrily, and out into the entrance hall. I shook her hand and said good-bye.

"I said more than I should have, more than I'm used to; I'm a bit scared of it. Why did I? But I need to talk. There are so many things I'd like to have an answer to, and I can't possibly know if you can answer any of them. I don't know you at all—or do I? I always feel I know immediately whether or not I like someone and whether they like me. It's a kind of electricity or magnetism or something; I've never studied psychology and that sort of thing. But I've been to psychiatrists and spent hours with them, and there wasn't much to gain from that, except I paid them to listen to me, and that's also getting something for your money. But the answers? Well, there are so many maybes. Why did I talk so much today of all days?"

"The ingenious idea behind the confessional is that it is anonymous."

"Anonymous? I don't feel you're anonymous."

"Well, shall we say, then, I played the role of a psychiatrist for a moment without being one. Thank God."

"You have something against psychiatrists?"

"Yes, but I can't give you any rational explanation for it. Except that if one is to gain anything from them, they should at least have more brains than oneself. That limits the supply!"

Mouse giggle.

"Oh, that's good, I have to remember that. Bye-bye!"

While I waited for the elevator she stood leaning up against the door frame, one knee bent up and pressed against the other and one arm stretched up along the jamb, the other on her waist to keep her robe together. She suddenly looked very lonely, though not her eyes, which were cheerful, but her body, which was so small, so forlorn, that it didn't want to say good-bye. But it had to. The upstretched arm waved to me, but as I was about to step into the elevator she thought of something and called after me:

"Your address, wait. Just write down your hotel and telephone number."

I barred the elevator door with my foot, tore a page out of my notebook, and wrote. She came over to me and stood close by me. I noticed her fragrance, a sweet fragrance from a warm body that soon would be made up; a fragrance of sleep and perfume from the day before, and something I couldn't define and which was all white and blue. I was shy and confused, and I said good-bye in a hurry, jumped into the elevator, and rode down. When the door closed, she said something, but I couldn't hear what it was. The fragrance was still in the car—and so was the voice and the eyes. When I got out on the street and began to walk back to my hotel, slowly and a bit dizzily, not even the faint warm evening breeze could air the fragrance out of me.

I am not superstitious, but—if I may be forgiven this, which even I find foolish—suddenly I feel that she is here in the room with me, that the many concentrated thoughts I have had of the past have reached her somewhere in infinity, pulled her, like a magnet, back through the lives that have been lived since it all took place, and into my room, where I am completely alone, in a house on a snow-covered ground. I feel that she is back, that she leans over my shoulder looking at the words that appear on the paper, and that she would do me harm if I committed sacrilege. Do biographers and chroniclers feel that way when they write about the dead? I listen for sounds, and inside myself a voice says out loud: Do you know how difficult you're making it for me

to write this story? Even though you said yourself that I
should write it sometime.

"Sometime?" I asked.

"When I'm dead."

"The whole story? Everything?"

She sat for a long time silently opposite me, thinking.
Her tongue ran over her lower lip. She looked as if she
had forgotten the question and were in some faraway
place.

"Marilyn!"

She returned with the speed of an electric shock, her
eyes became very wide and very happy, and her smile,
like a liberation, lit up her whole face—that strange,
strange smile: It undressed her face and the nakedness
spread out over her. Her smile always came as a surprise,
almost as a shock; it was like seeing a little, innocent,
naked schoolgirl suddenly smiling the smile of a grown,
mature, and very sophisticated woman.

"Yes, everything; I'll risk it. If you write it truthfully,
they won't say I was a beast, even though I have been
sometimes. You're a poet, so you can write the truth,
can't you? Actually, I've had enough of writers; yes,
them, too. If you don't write the truth, you'll live to regret
it."

"It'll be the most difficult task of my life."

"Thank you, darling, that was a compliment. No, it
wasn't a compliment; it was love!"

But the truth—where is it? It always seems to be somewhere behind the apparent truth, and the constant delv-
ing into a new, different, and deeper reality can never
stop. It may also be necessary to conceal, to change the
identity of living persons so that they may be more correctly described, which is only possible if one takes the
liberty of putting masks over their outward faces.

Do you understand that?

Do you understand that this is what I've been forced to do? That Fred's real name and appearance were different and that your secretary, who came to see me the day after, looked different and had another name than the one I've given her in this story? You had no wish to unveil them, and they themselves have chosen to be silent, to be content with their own memories. But it is no sacrilege if I don't render all remarks exactly as they were said—which I wouldn't be able to, anyway, since I didn't write anything down. It would have hurt and disappointed you deeply if you had seen me suddenly taking notes of what you said and did. All confidence would have evaporated, and we would have lost one another instantly.

It's all true anyway, isn't it?

Yes, but—won't the story lack credence that way?

I don't feel it will. I can't come any closer than that. You see now? It is a difficult task.

I have only one answer, the one you gave yourself: It is done out of love for you. You're right. The story isn't meant to be a compliment to you; it is not a detective story, not a reportage. It is an attempt to throw some of the light that came from the eyes that saw back into the darkness in which your mind was traveling. I am not a criminologist trying to find the guilty and the innocent but a very young person who today has become old and who wants to try to describe joy and grief, life and non-life. This attempt, of course, was unknown to me when I walked, a young man, northward on Second Avenue and the yellow, dented taxis rattled by and the long, black limousines glided along to their wealthy addresses. I had experienced a wonder. I was dizzy and confused and quite amazed. Well, poor thing! It was excusable, considering my age and Marilyn's—and it's true—she was fluorescent; everything and everybody around her was transformed into light directed toward her, which she returned in another color—the color of skin, light-blue eyes, moist-red mouth, silver-shine hair. Time and again I asked myself why on earth she had bothered to talk to ME. I'm not very different from everybody else. But maybe everybody else isn't very different from me either. That was no answer. And then all the men who must have felt the same, whom she had made into mirrors to reflect herself while they hopelessly sank into paralyzing ecstasy—men who were famous, handsome, and rich, none of which I was. Nor could I be of any advantage to her career; well, yes, there was the film idea and the agent's interest, and perhaps I had some talent, but who knew if it would ever manage to come through, to become art that rose above the stream of agreeable, good writing and politely received indifference? Why me of all people? Well, tomorrow she would have forgotten me. It was just one afternoon's madness, an amusing little experiment in diving down into the anonymous masses that from infinite distance gazed at her, the star, and I was one of those gazers.

Now, with hindsight, I could have told myself that she was at the time one of the loneliest people in all the human swarm of America. And loneliness often leads to the most unpredictable meetings.

I remember that I had some ideas about an aura. But it sounded all too conceited, and I ended up going into a bar asking for a double straight Scotch and thinking it was all just a curious coincidence; tomorrow everything would be forgotten, and I would have a sweet, vibrant memory which finally would become a dusty page in a diary, well hidden in the attic of a long life.

But it happened quite differently. Now I sit here at the desk in the house on the windswept island, the unforested island where the few trees bend toward the east and the *wind pulls at the thatched roof so the rafters emit long, creaking sounds. And I try to remember; I dig like an archeologist into old cellars, deep down into the mass of my brain, and as more shards come up all the time, I become still a bit more superstitious and vulnerable and skinless and oversensitive, and I find the fragrance of her. The touch steals into my hands, and I remember she once said about herself and a good friend of hers, who was a famous film star, that "we attract others like the colors of flowers attract bees, and we cannot defend ourselves against them any more than the flowers can. They are at anybody's mercy, and once in a while parasites come along and eat at us, and we try to close ourselves but we can't, because then we couldn't act anymore. If you want to be a great actor you have to let yourself be eaten and covered with wounds by the ones who bite . . ."*

I shut my eyes almost entirely so that my long room widens and becomes obscure in its boundlessness. My bed is at the other end of the room; it is not made. I don't want to waste time cleaning and keeping things orderly; nobody comes to inspect whether I keep a decent orderly house, so I don't. And I see her lying in the pile of quilts and pillows on the bed, stretching her bare arms up around her face, and her head is very small and her hair wildly disheveled like quicksilver running after itself to be unified, yet shaking apart all the time, and her body is half turned under the quilt, so as to intimate the high arc of her hip.

"Come talk to me," she says.

"Can't you sleep?"

"You know I can't. I can never sleep."

5th Day

In the morning I was roused by the telephone, which stood on the night table and rang me awake.

"There's a lady who wants to talk to you," said the desk clerk.

"Who . . . who is it?"

"The 'lady' doesn't wish to state her name. Don't you think I asked?"

"Oh, of course."

"I certainly hope so, sir. Here she is."

It wasn't her. But I recognized the voice; it was the secretary's. She spoke in a subdued tone as if someone were near who wasn't supposed to hear what she was talking about.

"I'd like to talk to you. It's very important. Could you manage it right away?"

"I can be ready in half an hour. Where do you want to meet? You're welcome to come to the hotel, but the receptionist . . ."

"No, thank you. There's a bar on the corner of Forty-second Street and United Nations Plaza. It has a respectable clientele who leave other guests alone. In half an hour?"

Nancy (I call her Nancy because that's about as far, alphabetically, as I can get from her real name) was there when I arrived. It was a dimly lit bar, and the tables were in separate bays—an excellent arrangement for people who didn't want to be seen or heard. She sat with her back to the entrance and as close to the wall as she could get. She looked up at me, still hostile, when I apologized for not getting there before she did. I asked what she would have. She wanted coffee. She remained silent until the coffee had been served and the waiter had gone. Meanwhile, she kept fidgeting with a paper napkin, rolling it up until it became as stiff as a stick.

"You must be wondering why I've arranged to see you," she said. "But there's something I have to tell you."

"Yes?"

She lifted her eyes from the hands wringing the napkin, and from within her hostility something beseeching suddenly sprang out.

"Won't you please keep away from Miss Monroe!"

I looked at her in surprise.

"Did she send you to me with that message?"

"No, she doesn't know I'm seeing you, and I must ask you not to tell her—and please don't tell her what I've said. Will you promise?"

I didn't answer.

"I hope you will, after I've told you what you have to know. Miss Monroe is in the middle of one of the worst depressions she's ever been through. She's also ill physically, and she's going to be hospitalized for a cure of her dependence on pills. It's absolutely necessary that she doesn't get involved in a new affair. I'm very,

very sorry that I'm forced to give you such confidential —and dangerous—information, but I just have no choice. I must trust in your goodwill that you won't use what I'm telling you against us."

"If, as you tell me, she's suffering a deep depression, she's hiding it pretty well."

"Do you imagine she is unable to do that?"

"If that depression is as serious as you're trying to tell me it is in this case, even a great actor couldn't cover it up."

"She's greater than the greatest."

"Her eyes are happy."

"Oh God, how little you know her. That's what's so unfortunate about it; you can't know what you're doing."

"I haven't tried to seduce her, and in all honesty, you don't really believe I have a chance of doing that?"

"Perhaps not. But I've known her for a long time. There aren't many who know her as well as I do, and I'm here to protect her. She needs someone to take care of her. And even though you may think as you say you do, I know that you've somehow insinuated yourself into her life."

"Now I must have a beer, if you don't mind. Coffee somehow doesn't fit the subject. Tell me, don't you think you're imagining all this?"

"No. I'm a level-headed woman, and I know what I'm talking about."

"I hope you believe me when I say that what you've just told me is more than surprising to me."

"Yes, that's precisely why I wanted to talk to you."

"And you don't think it should be left up to Miss Monroe herself to decide what she wants?"

"No, because she can't. She's too naïve for that. I don't mean that in any derogatory sense; it's a beautiful quality. But it's an easy way to get hurt. And that's what it has led to many times. You will soon discover that for yourself. And then you'll try the same as all the others—to 'save' her; everybody wants to save her, and it only makes things worse. Unfortunately, there are too many saviors who have ulterior motives. She's so easy to take advantage of—for your own benefit."

"As I'm sure you know, my connection with Miss Monroe is merely a result of the fact that both she and Fred are interested in the synopsis and the film project that I've suggested to them. You can hardly blame me if I'm proud and happy over that interest. And how that should be an expression of a secretly evil intent, I don't think even you could convince me."

"There are plenty of film projects—more than enough. But there's no possibility that she'll go through with any of them. She's signed up long ago for much more work during the next year than her health will ever allow her to perform. Some want to get her into a big TV production, others want to push her into a Broadway theater. They're the craziest. She could never go through with it, and she can't survive a flop —either artistically or in her private life. I don't really doubt your goodwill, and I understand very well how you feel and that all this must sound quite extraordinary to you—but I'm sure you've heard rumors."

"No, but I'm possibly also suffering a bit of naïveté, and it's probably not as beautiful as Miss Monroe's. I actually haven't yet understood what it is that you want to tell me. Don't you think you'd better explain? I can't promise you that I'll keep our talk a secret if Miss Monroe asks me directly, and you shouldn't demand that of me, but I have no intention of broadcasting anything. I hope you believe that."

She remained silent, sitting with her head bent, and

suddenly she began to unroll the napkin and dry her eyes with it. When she looked up at me again there were still tears in her eyes, and everything was changed.

"There's a horde of reporters after us," she said, "to get material for their gossip columns. You don't know the conditions we have to live under when there's something we have to hide. What I'm telling you now you could sell for a lot of money."

"But you don't think I would dream of doing that, do you?"

"No. Not anymore. Miss Monroe's . . ."

"Excuse me, just one more thing. You mustn't demand the impossible of me . . . even though I don't yet know myself what the impossible is. You understand what I mean?"

"Yes. But I have no choice. I do it only for Marilyn's sake. I love her so much. She wants so much, including much that she can't manage, and what she can manage she doesn't want. She's a unique person, a very very great talent. She's warm and wants so much to help others, but she blocks herself . . . The ambition, the energy that clashes, her frightful insomnia, abuse of pills, alcohol . . . She's misunderstood and stepped on and misused, forced into wrong roles . . . She gets bad advice, and she follows it. She gets herself into impossible situations because of her strong temperament, because she's a perfectionist and knows more about the art of film than anybody else. She turns herself inside out to please others, then suddenly rebels against it and makes vicious enemies who can easily hurt her deeply. And they do because they don't understand her. She's the dearest, she's a child, and she's much more intelligent than anybody thinks. She's more full of contradictions than any person I've met, and there are millstones grinding in her; they're grinding away her self-assurance, her taste for life, into pulp. She can't bear that anything living be killed, she believes even flowers have a soul, but in her most desperate situations she herself would like to die. She has at the same time a great talent for life and an urge for death, and everything gets blown into bits and pieces in her mind. Her marriage is over. There are rumors about it, but they both want to hide it. She has a great need to be alone just now, but at the same time she's desperate over living alone, that her marriage didn't work out—that on top of everything else. She's so much wanted to have children, but she can't; it goes wrong every time. It makes her think she's unworthy, and yet she can shine and play her own myth and have an unrestrained belief in a new project—all too uncritically. She's drifting in the wind; she's a very pretty ship, but she has no rudder. I have a feeling—though I'm not sure—that her husband still believes the marriage can be saved; he's so inscrutable. While she opens up without resistance, he slams himself shut, but I believe he still has great love for her. He doesn't know that anything has happened to make her through with him; he's already out of her life, not outwardly but . . . Excuse me, this all sounds terribly confused; I didn't want to say it this way, it's more difficult than I thought . . . But if she doesn't get a long rest and psychiatric help, I really fear the worst. The pills, the sleeping pills, I can't tell you how terrible it is to watch it, to try to help and not be able to, to be powerless when you feel you have only one role in life—to help her. And then, suddenly, she can be so happy, so much in love, so vital in the midst of this doped-up self-destruction. I'm swimming with a human being in my arms, a human being who's about to drown in an endless ocean . . ."

6th Day

I didn't know what to do. I wandered around Manhattan but found no joy in things I otherwise would have enjoyed. The city was rapidly warming up for the summer, but I didn't notice it. I tried to do further work on the first draft of the film script but I couldn't.

I bought a few movie books and proceeded to stare at her pictures in them. I saw something different in them that I hadn't seen before: sadness, anxiety, longing. But the smiling eroticism, so apparently simple, was there too. The joy in being photographed, in being looked at and admired, was there. The intensity of a sought-after and worked-on posture was there. And there was devotion, sweetness, come-closer, touch-me, it's-all-just-a-pleasure-and-joy-to-me. But then again: What is it I've lost? Where am I to go? Will somebody please find me? I've been lost.

Many times I was on my way to Fred's office, but I turned around and never went up. I went over to Fifty-seventh Street and looked up at her windows, then went away again.

7th Day

The telephone rang. I woke up immediately. I always wake up at the slightest noise. It was a quarter past two in the morning.

"It's a lady, sir. It's not the same one, but she won't give her name either. Excuse me, sir, but do you only have lady friends with no names?"

"Yes, that's my specialty."

"May I suggest that you get all your ladies with no names christened. It's customary in the States to be christened."

"Actually, they're all Americans."

"Impossible. Americans are a respectable Christian people."

"All of them?"

"All right, almost all. I'm sorry you seem to meet only the exceptions. Would you please tell the lady that she shouldn't call this late at night."

"Tell me, are you the night porter, too?"

"For the prices we get at this hotel we can't afford

a night porter. In return, we expect our guests to show a little consideration. This is not a nightclub."

"My dear Mr. Receptionist, I'm well aware of that."

"And I'm nobody's 'dear,' sir."

"I'm aware of that, too."

"Are you also aware, sir, when you'll be leaving?"

"No, how do you like that? That's something I'm not aware of! Now, how about connecting me with the lady who has no name?"

"Maybe you haven't been christened either?"

"Yes, I have been, unfortunately. But I was only three months old at the time, so I couldn't protest. Would you be kind enough to put the lady through?"

"How can you know who it is if you don't know her name?"

"I'm clairvoyant."

"I might as well tell you that we don't want any ghosts in the hotel."

"You may rest assured that she doesn't look anything like a ghost, and she isn't either. Perhaps you would . . ."

"Here you are."

Click.

That desk clerk. He was very big and very fat and very pale. His head was made of dough. The one job he should never have had was that of a desk clerk at a hotel. He should have been a police officer in the Bowery. What sobering up he could have accomplished! But we always get into the wrong positions. I remember just after I arrived I discovered that the prongs of my electric shaver didn't fit the outlet; I needed flat prongs, not round ones. I went down to the receptionist and asked if he had a converter.

"A converter! What on earth makes you think I

would have a converter? We don't deal in electrical supplies."

"Look here, I can't possibly be the first European to have stayed in this hotel. Others must have had the same problem many times."

"If you don't like the States, then go home."

"As it happens, I've just arrived, and I don't care to travel to Europe every time I have to shave."

"What?"

"Is there a place in the neighborhood where I can buy a converter?"

"Try an antique shop."

It was her.

"Did I wake you?"

"It doesn't matter. I'm glad you called. How are you?"

"I can't sleep; I have to talk to someone. Are you up for talking?"

"Sure, all night."

"You're sweet. I knew it. And you probably don't snore either."

"No. At least, that's what I'm told."

"How do you sleep? On your back or on your side?"

"On my side. But if I take a nap during the day, I have to do it on my back. It's stupid, but that's how it is. At night, I can only sleep on my side."

"I sleep on my stomach—most of the time, at any rate. I just read some good poems by cummings; you know him? He's good—even if I don't understand all of it. He's just good."

"Yes, I once wrote a novel in which the heroine was modeled on a stanza by cummings."

"Really? That's wonderful. How did it go?"

I recited:

"My girl's tall with hard long eyes
as she stands, with her long hard hands keeping
silence on her dress, good for sleeping
is her long hard body filled with surprise
like a shocking wire—"

"Oh, that's beautiful. That's not the way I am. I'm short and fat and soft. But I can be easily filled with surprise—much more so than people think. Well, no, that wasn't the meaning of the poem. I don't have long legs; mine are too short. I've always had a lot of trouble with them."

"One can be beautiful in many ways. You've found one of them."

"Thank you. You're sweet. Very, very sweet. Who is your favorite author?"

"I have two. They're very different on the surface but only on the surface: Hemingway and Camus."

"Hemingway! I don't like him. He's always killing. He kills everything. One shouldn't kill anything living. He's a roughneck."

She became silent, and I had time to think about her voice. It was drowsy and yet strong; there was a tense alertness behind the sleepiness.

"Do you suffer from insomnia?" I asked.

"A writer is something more than himself," she said. "Like an actor. If he's good he becomes a hero to lots of people. That puts him under an obligation. Hemingway makes millions of people admire death. That's wrong. It's immoral. One should make people believe in love—in living. That's the first time we haven't agreed. How's Camus?"

"He writes about living—about surviving."

"That's better. I'll go down tomorrow and buy everything they have by him. I'm afraid of death. Maybe it's because I'm afraid of old age. I can get sick over every day that passes. I grow uglier. You should see my hands; they're getting old already."

"They say age can be a gift if you don't resist it. If you go along, it's like swimming with the tide, it makes many things easier."

"I don't understand that. Why?"

"Maybe because you stop fighting what's immaterial."

"I wish it were that way. But that's not how it is with me. I should get wiser; things should get easier, as you say, but they don't. Can you be born immature? I mean, can you have a gene or something in you that simply makes you unable to mature?"

"Is that the way you feel about yourself?"

Silence.

"You ask very intimate questions."

"You encourage it. Anyway, if they aren't intimate, they're immaterial."

Another silence.

"I don't want to hurt you. Have I?" I asked.

"No, I know you don't want to hurt me. But you make me think. Do you believe I'm not as happy as I appear to be?"

(Nancy?)

"All I believe so far is that you're a good many things at once."

"Seems to me I was better off when I was younger. I've become suspicious. But I act as if I weren't. Hold on a moment, I just have to change my position. There. Are you still there?"

"How about your ear?"

"I always use the same ear; I'm a bit deaf in one. But you're right; it begins to hum, as if I were about to bust something in it. I said I had become suspicious; what

41

else can you be in my business? I can assure you I've met some real stinkers. But you never know when it's just play-acting and when not—not in your own case or with others."

"Well, that, too, is a realization that supposedly comes with age. It may be useful."

"You mean I've learned to smell them at a distance?"

"Yes, among other things."

"It's gotten me into some impossible situations. And I've been wrong, too. I can't figure it out. Do you know my mother ended up in a mental hospital?"

"No. Is she still alive?"

Silence. A long silence.

"Yes. I've lied about it. It was the movie company that got me to do it. But I've admitted it was a lie. Why do I always let them talk me into it? Why am I so insecure? It's as if I couldn't keep up with my own body. It grows older but *I* don't. Is that a sign of insanity?"

"No. Everybody feels that now and then—until one day mind and body come together again."

"Really? Are you sure? You're not old enough to know that; you're just saying it to comfort me. You're no older than I am, so how could you know a thing like that?"

"So let's say I believe it's that way."

"That wasn't fair."

"Well, then I *do* know it."

"You're clever—very clever at evasion. We won't discuss it anymore. I don't want to quarrel with you. I'll try to believe you're right and that you have a secret place where you get information no one else has. You're sleepy now, aren't you? Do you want to go to sleep?"

"No. I'd like to talk to you all night. In fact, there's nothing I'd like more."

"That's not true."

"There you are: full of suspicion. Stop that."

"I can't figure it out."

"What can't you figure out?"

"Anything."

"That doesn't sound like you're going to sleep any better now."

"No, I can't, I can't. But I'd like to talk to you more. There's something I don't know. Shall we meet tomorrow?"

"Sure. Where?"

"Not here. There's a little bar ten steps down the street on the left-hand side when you're coming from your hotel. Shall we say two o'clock tomorrow?"

"By all means. But they'll recognize you; they won't leave us alone."

She laughed that little laughter that was more smile than sound.

"Not even you will recognize me. Sleep well—and say hello to the desk man for me. I don't think he liked me."

"He doesn't like me either."

"So move to another hotel."

"No, because actually I like him. But he doesn't care for ladies—especially those who call after two in the morning. But please do it again. It's good for him to get used to it. He'll be happy to be confirmed in his belief that all corruption comes from Europe."

"Tell me, aren't you a bit crazy yourself?"

"Of course; everybody is. We're all a bit cracked, a bit prosaic, a bit spoilt, and a bit puritanical."

"You mean we're all alike."

"That's not what I said. The ingredients may be very differently proportioned. But they're all there."

"You're quite sure of that?"

43

"Yes."

"And I thought I was something special."

"You can still be special, even though you're like everybody else, too."

"I don't understand that, but maybe it's because I'm getting sleepy. Talking to you is almost like getting a massage. It's the best sleep medicine I know. Do you mean everything you've said to me?"

"Yes."

"Are you always so sure of yourself?"

"No."

"Thank God. Good night, then. See you."

Click.

At the same moment the neon sign facing the hotel, proclaiming "Schlitz, the beer that made Milwaukee famous," went out, and my room got dark. I fell asleep in the sudden New York darkness. But on my way to sleep the questions flashed through my brain: Is Nancy telling the truth? If not, what is she after?

Who is the swimmer and who the drowning one?

Are there shores one can't see?

8th Day

I was in the bar at the prearranged time; she hadn't arrived. It was a bar à la Nancy, though not quite so. People came here to drink. It was not a bar for politicians and diplomats but for those who wanted to enjoy their drink in peace, and if they wished to talk, nobody disturbed them. But it was just as dimly lit as Nancy's bar and similarly divided into bays. It was safer, too; nobody would dream of seeing Marilyn Monroe turn up here. And nobody did. She came a half-hour late, in unpressed beige slacks, a white shirt somewhat crumpled, a beige kerchief snug around her hair, no makeup at all, and large sunglasses—a bag dangling, teenaged fashion, from her shoulder. I stood up and waved to her, and nobody noticed her as she walked through the bar toward me. She was pale. I couldn't see through the dark glasses to tell if she had shadows under her eyes, but she appeared as if she did. Judging by her looks, she wasn't feeling well; something was wrong, and it could hardly be her insomnia alone. The lively, amusing girl

45

from the telephone the night before was gone; this was a different one. She wanted gin and tonic.

She quickly emptied the first glass and said yes to another.

"Arthur has written a screenplay from 'The Misfits.' Do you know it?"

"The short story, yes."

"He's rewritten it so there'll be a part in it for me. I'd like to play it, and I don't want to. It'll give me the chance to show that I can *act*—not just the dumb blonde, but really act. He thinks it can save our marriage. I can't tell him that it can't. That's something he just doesn't understand and I can't say. He's always been good to me, but it's also been hell sometimes. Look, I'm doing it again; you wouldn't know anything about it. Why do I act as if you did?"

She turned the empty glass between her nervous fingers.

"You want one more—even though we'll get a bit drunk, or perhaps very drunk? And tell me whatever you want—all you want. And if I ask questions you don't care to answer, then don't. It's not absolutely necessary that people join forces just because they've met on a deserted island."

"You would like to make your film, and you want me to play the lead because it'll make you famous and earn you a lot of money. Don't you think I know that? You're no different from the others."

"Of course. That can't come as a surprise to you. But if you don't want to, or if you can't, it's all right with me; we won't be enemies because of that. In any case, you wouldn't have to let that bother you. Let's talk about something else."

For a moment she took off her glasses and looked at me to see if I was putting on an act—an act she knew in all its nuances. She did have shadows under her eyes.

"I can't decide whether to believe you or not," she said, putting her glasses back on. "I'm sorry, I don't feel well today. You're not the usual kind of cheek-kisser, but you're not quite indifferent to me either, are you?"

"I think of you all day and part of the night, too. That will hardly surprise you. But making or not making a film is not the be-all and end-all, except perhaps while it's in the making. After all, I'm old enough to know it's not the most important thing in the world."

"What is the most important thing in the world?"

"Love."

"Are you sure there is any? I mean . . . No, I can't express it. I, too, have experienced it, but it never comes off. I've been married four times, did you know that?"

"No, I knew of three."

"I've never talked about it to anyone, and I don't want to. 'Cause they're always writing about me but never the right things. Is that my own fault because I'm not good enough at explaining it as it really was?"

"If people wrote their own interviews—I mean both the questions and the answers—the world would look quite different. It would be more true, more sympathetic. An interview can't be any better than the journalist who does it; that's the trouble for those who have something to say. Besides, people are always being asked the wrong questions. So, they usually give the wrong answers."

"Oh, that's true; that's exactly how it is. Sometimes I write poems. They're not worth anything, of course, but they're right. Do you write poems?"

"Yes, but they're not worth anything either. They are right, however—for me."

"You don't look like a failure of any sort. You're unspoilt. So how can you say what you're saying?"

"That, on the other hand, I can't answer. Another drink?"

"Mmm!"

"Listen, I know I'm not familiar with your circumstances, your feelings, your background—whatever it is that forces you into a role you apparently want to get out of—but there are some facts: You're beautiful, you're the biggest star there is; any film company knows that a movie you're in will make lots of money. You're young. You've got every opportunity open to you. You can choose what you want. It simply has to be possible to make it all fit into a pattern that you can live in and be glad you're a part of."

"I'm far less free than you think. I bought the books I could get by Camus. One of them is called *The Rebel*. Was that the one you wanted me to read?"

"Yes, that's one of them. First you should read his novels and short stories and essays. After that *The Rebel* will make much more sense. There's a sentence in it that goes like this: 'We all carry within us our places of exile, our crimes, and our ravages. But our task is not to unleash them on the world; it is to fight them in ourselves and in others.' "

She took off her sunglasses, looked around—there was nobody near—leaned forward to me across the table, impulsively seized my hand, and held it in hers.

"It may be that I'm a bit drunk now, and I know and don't know what I want to say, but I feel it's very important—good God, isn't it though? I both want and don't want to do what I do. When I meet people who are strong—and also when they're weak—I reflect them; I make myself their moon. And I feel myself disappear while I stand there and cast off their light. Or I may experience it differently: I'm taking part in a race in which I didn't want to participate in the first place, but somebody has made me do it; and yet I also want to, in order to win—even though I feel I'll fall and die before I reach the finish line. And while I'm running the race and straining, I'm thinking I want to drop out of it and never run anymore. But I don't do it; the others force me to continue, or they have captured that part of me that wants to continue. Or maybe I'm just terribly ashamed to do anything they don't expect me to do, so I run and die a little all the time. But they mustn't see it—and I don't believe they do see it either—so my rebellion never becomes anything more than insomnia and a quick rage and meaningless kicks at those who want to help me; and at the same time I'd like to be nice to them. But I find myself suddenly in a situation where I really am a 'monster,' even though I don't want to be. I don't always think only of myself. I've admired people, had my idols—I've been married to one of them— but they don't live up to my expectations, or they misunderstand me and want to change me. And they succeed. But when they've changed me I don't love them anymore. You said love was the most important thing in the world. What's most important is that *I* love, not that I'm loved—you understand? I'm really a misfit!"

9th Day

In the afternoon a messenger brought a letter to my hotel. She had hand-written it with a narrow-point pen in a nervous hand, most of the lines drooping but individual words taking small leaps upward. She quoted a line from Camus: "The immortality of the soul preoccupies many good brains. But that is because they deny the only truth given to them, their own body, even before they have used up its vitality and strength." She apologized for talking up all of our time together with talking about her own problems rather than discussing my project. And she ciosed by inviting me to a party she would be giving for some of her friends the following evening.

10th Day

I was delayed by a telephone call from Europe; a foreign publisher I knew well needed some information in connection with a translation of a book of mine, and I didn't want to offend him by cutting the conversation short. The apartment was full of guests when I arrived. Somewhere in the cluster of blue and striped jackets and bare shoulders she stood with a filled champagne glass, flashing with silver and white. I was seeing her for the first time as the world saw her. She was no longer short and a bit chubby, and thanks to a perfect makeup job the pale face and the lumpy nose were gone; her eyelashes were longer, her eyes larger, and the mousy laughter was there no more. She gesticulated and beamed, and her laughter was more open. This was the princess surrounded by her court, and she enjoyed it; they all looked as if they were dancing around a Christmas tree, fully trimmed and lit. In her white dress she looked long-legged and slender and beautiful. Silver threads were sewn into the white lace, so it looked as if melted silver were running down over her and billowing back up over her again, up to her hair, which I was seeing for the first time. It was set thick and smooth down along her face and doubled back around her neck, while curls came down over her forehead to the boldly drawn eyebrows; her lips were a red lantern. She was the loveliest creature I'd ever seen, and I thought: She is *light*—a light that comes from inside her, a roving spotlight blinding everyone who looks at her, so that they experience her only as radiance, the myth as a nonhuman wonder behind the vibrant erotic human being. And the beauty of her face contained the belief of a very young, hopeful, vibrant, shy but happy girl that soon, oh soon, she would have her hopes of joy come true . . . I didn't know anybody among those I saw, and I remained standing at the door unsure of what to do. I would have liked to go over to her but I didn't. I was hopelessly outside it all, but I was satisfied with my ticket to the balcony where I could enjoy watching as if it were all a film from the distant world of wealth, beauty, and fame. In a little while I would sneak away, finally realizing that I had approached a planet where ordinary earthlings were not allowed . . . I shook my head over my own foolish presumption, my hubris, which could only be properly rewarded with a mocking laughter. What did I imagine? But suddenly she was gliding through the blue sea of friends and hangers-on, and the billows of shoulders parted before her, and she came right up to me.

"There you finally are, Hans. Why were you so late?"

(How on earth had she noticed that?)

"Here!"

She gave me her glass of champagne.

"Take it, I'll find myself another. It's Dom Perignon, my favorite champagne."

"How are you, Miss Magnet?" I heard myself say.

She was standing very close to me and looked me unmercifully in the eyes.

"*M . . . M* again, eh? It must be because you write poetry. You know I really should have been called Jean Monroe. Did you ever think about why it's harder to change your first name than your surname? Or Norma Monroe, perhaps? But everything was always decided for me by others. It was 20th Century–Fox that named me—and who goes against the gods, as long as you believe they're gods?"

"You don't believe that anymore?"

"They're real devils, and that may be just about the same. Come, you have to say hello to my friends."

I went the round but couldn't hear what they said, and nobody caught my name, which also was immaterial, and I ended up on a sofa at the center of a heated discussion between a white-haired gentleman, whom I later understood was a well-known lyric poet, and a bespectacled historian, who apparently had made a name for himself in U.S. intellectual circles. I refrained from following her with my eyes, though I could see that she looked at me a few times, because I felt it was inappropriate that anybody should believe that I knew her in a special way. I thought I should do my best to be as inconspicuous as possible and remember what I had recognized just a while before—that I was Mr. Nobody Dane.

"The United States is the genuine socialistic society," said the white-haired poet. "We have succeeded in creating the perfect group life, an idolized bureaucratization of each and every person, not through outside pressure but because we ourselves, each of us, not only accept it but wish it; we want nothing more than to fit in, and when we feel we do, completely and entirely, we're happy, and we fit our ideal. It's the only time in world history that a collective has been successfully created by free choice."

The historian shook his spectacles in dismay. In fact, he sometimes had two pairs on at the same time:

"Quite the contrary. What is happening in the United States today is a rebellion against our way of life, a revolution which in range and force will far surpass what the Russian Revolution ever achieved. It only changed the outward circumstances; the Russian people remained the same. Don't believe that a thousand years' schooling in humility is the same as acceptance."

The white-haired one also shook his mane very dismayed and spilled champagne—Dom Perignon?—on his well-pressed pants.

"Where do you get that nonsense from? Some silly students at Harvard? You of all people should be able to recognize that the total *inner* socialism has been our way of life for a long time. Instruction in the asocial intellectual fields is being dropped everywhere, and instead we base instruction in all grades on the indoctrination of social understanding and sociability and adaptation to the community. Today, we look at the introvert, the self-probing, with suspicion. We take pride in giving up our private independence in favor of the group. It reaches up to the most elevated of sciences and proves to give the most brilliant results: a superior unity of inner peace and outer solidarity, which is the prerequisite of the greatest possible efficiency."

"You can't seriously believe that the individualism that created America could have disappeared that quickly? It's still there, though under certain circumstances it may give the appearance of collaboration because we recognize the necessity of it. But we experience that as a dictatorship, however imperceptible and

benevolent it may be, and the rebellion against it will erupt politically, artistically—everywhere—in a few years."

I said something, but they didn't hear it, and it was probably hopeless, too—old-fashioned European. In fact, I couldn't recognize any of the aspects of my own existence, which wasn't anything new or earth-shattering either.

Then Marilyn sat down on the arm of the sofa and asked if she could join the conversation.

The two disputants raised their voices and looked at her once in a while, gesturing in her direction with their hands, but neither of them dreamed of asking her a question. It was like watching a play with two old professionals who had said the same things in a hundred performances. She bent down to me and whispered in my ear:

"Why don't you look at me? Anyway, you're supposed to dance with your hostess the first time you're a guest in her house."

"Well, but . . ."

"So dance with me."

We immediately found each other's rhythm. She enjoyed dancing. I held her tightly, and she was soft and pliable and knew in advance every step I took. She put her cheek against mine and whispered:

"Some of them are so smart they don't make any sense. The others are not at all. But they've fooled me all my life. I've tried to learn something from them; I'd like to learn; I know practically nothing. But they talk to me like medicine men and witch doctors, and I pretend to understand them, but I don't."

"It doesn't necessarily make much difference."

"No? I'd so much like to be smarter. Then I wouldn't be so suspicious."

"You're alive."

"Yes, at this moment; at this moment."

We danced past a bottle of champagne and some glasses standing on a shelf. She let go of me, took the bottle, and poured, so the champagne flowed over from both glasses, ran off the shelf, and down to the floor. She lifted her glass and we toasted, and at that moment a cold puff of air came our way; someone had opened a window, and the smoke cleared. She took my hand and pulled me into another room, over to the open window, where the breeze came in off the East River and lifted her hair.

"I know what it is I want to achieve," she said. "But I can't explain it. Or rather, if I do, it sounds bad."

"Become a great actress, greater than anyone else?"

"Mnnnh! But also be happy. The trouble is the two things don't go together. Or can they? You're a poet; you explain it to me."

"Have you ever wished you were a tree, a very beautiful tree that everybody admired but still just a tree?"

"Yes, how did you know?"

"Because it is both things at the same time."

She turned to me, kissed me on the cheek, and took a deep breath of the fresh air.

"I understand what you're trying to say, but I can't explain what it is that I understand. I've also wanted to be a bird. Maybe I was a bird in a former life; I recognize so much of myself when I see them in Central Park. But when I leave them and go back to my own life, I'm not happy anymore. I'm still a bird, but I'm captive in a cage, and I'm scared out of my wits, and I dream of breaking out through the bars and soaring up, up, up . . . Sometimes at night I dream I become free and fly up toward the sun and into it, so my wings burn off and I fall back through the universe . . . Are you sure there aren't birds that die that way? I also have another dream—that I'm in church and I get up during the sermon and take all my clothes off and stand there naked, and they all look at me terror-stricken. Is there any connection between the two dreams? Have you discovered anything in me that you didn't know before?"

She didn't wait for an answer but left me and walked away from the window, disappearing among the voices, the music, and the smoke. I followed slowly, found myself a corner and hid, so no one saw me. Again, I most wanted to leave, but I knew there was something she wanted to tell me. So I stayed.

Shortly before midnight the party broke up. Somebody clapped his hands, and I understood that it had been decided to go out to see someone everybody appeared to know, somewhere on Long Island.

Cars were provided, and I stood behind a confused group of people who didn't know in what car they should go because they couldn't make up their minds with whom they most wanted to be, until she took me firmly by the arm and pulled me into a car. We sat in the back seat, behind a very talkative married couple. The man was the driver. They were turning around all the time, talking to Marilyn about common acquaintances. I felt her hip and her shoulder next to me, although the back seat was broad, and I crossed my arms so that my elbow hid my hand and groped in the dark. She was there, and she found my hand without the others' seeing it, took hold of two of my fingers, and ran her thumb exploringly over and between my knuckles, up over my hand along the veins to my wrist, trying to discover every bump and dent, stroking my hand as lightly and deliberately as if the soft skin of her thumb were drawing a string of kisses over my skin. We deceived the others, knowing that we were hidden in the dark, and smiled mysteriously because nobody suspected what we were doing, but we didn't look at one another and we didn't talk together. She camouflaged us with quick answers which sounded as if she were interested. We drove along nearly deserted turnpikes, and finally we were out among trees and large villas and could occasionally glimpse the sea and the silvery shore in the moonlight. We drove in a black-and-white negative until we turned into a stately driveway and stopped in front of a palatial mansion with lights in every window and people moving in slow motion across them. We stepped out and went together up the broad front steps; it smelled of sea and honeysuckle and wet grass and caraway. Inside, the whole ceremony was repeated —embraces, shouts of welcome, and short introductions. I followed in her wake like a dinghy no one took any notice of, and I didn't catch the host's name either, but he slapped me on the shoulder and left me leaning up against the bar. My silvery lighthouse of a girl beamed among the blue and striped jackets and the pale shoulders in the whiteness of a ballroom with a background of tall, dark windows. The French doors stood open, and I could hear the sea close by, flowing in slow, long waves up toward the house. There were faces around me that I recognized, and somebody said something to me; I replied politely and was left alone. I followed her with my eyes without anybody noticing it, and I was filled with an impish happiness but made an effort to look nonchalant. I had a Scotch and another and then one more and waited because there was still something she wanted with me.

Finally, she came and said she wanted to go down to the beach. Without touching each other we quickly went through the balcony door and down a long flight of steps. In an extension of the mansion-palace there were two swimming pools at different levels like two postcards from the Aegean Sea. The next thing we knew we were on the beach by the sea, and we took each other's hands and walked down to the water's edge while the sounds of the party became garbled like the transmission from a radio station that is about to sign off. We reached the edge of the water and stood there quietly watching the sea and the broad band of moonlight on the waves, which looked like pods of frolicking seals. And we listened to the stillness that stretched around us like a sleeping hand that opens in a dream, and she bent down and took her shoes off—she wasn't wearing any stockings—pulled her white dress up around her legs, and went a few feet out into the water.

"I love the sea," she said. "Isn't it strange? It's endless, it's dangerous, but I always feel so secure and free when I'm by the sea. The sea is the most beautiful memory I have from my childhood. Come . . ."

I took off my shoes and socks and pulled up my trousers. I took her hand, and we walked away from the house with the long, black, lacquer-smooth waves washing around our legs. The waves broke on us; she pulled her dress farther up and went out deeper, and I gave up on my trousers and let them get wet; I didn't give a damn. We glided through the water like two unlit smuggler ships on their way to a secret cove on the desolate shore—to the dark houses and trees, which all were hunched a little landward. Far behind us the party was shining, and finally the water was up above her knees, and she stopped and laughed, threw her arms around my neck, then let go of me, and went quickly ashore. She planted herself in front of me with her dress up around her hips and stuck out her bare leg, telling me to dry it.

I found my handkerchief and went down on my knees in front of her, dried her wet leg, wrung the handkerchief, and dried again. I saw that her legs were not so long and pretty as everybody thought; they were funny; they were cute; they were hard inside, behind the softness. Then came the other leg. I didn't dare look up at her; I was hopelessly old-fashioned and shy, and when I got up with her shoes, which she had thrown down beside her, in my hand, she put her arms around me, and we kissed. She lifted herself on tiptoe, and we fit snugly together, and her mouth was open and smooth like the sea.

We walked back, and at the bottom of the steps I helped her put her shoes on, brushed my irredeemably wet, sand-covered trousers, and struggled to get into my own shoes, which had become too small. We went up the steps and were about to enter the ballroom when she quickly took my arm and stopped me, pulled my handkerchief out of my breast pocket, where it hung all bulky and wet, and wiped my mouth.

"Do I have to do everything myself, silly?" she said, gave me back my handkerchief, and entered the room alone.

I waited long enough for nobody to suspect that we had been together, hurried through the ballroom, and sat down at the far end of the bar, hiding my wet, crumpled, and slightly shrunk trouser legs under the bar stool. I felt some water seep down into my shoes, which became still smaller and pinched like hell, and downed another couple of Scotches in order to get the cold out of my feet. I couldn't help grinning to myself; I had come to write the script of a comedy about "a European in New York," and bang!—here it all was: the lavish wealth, the self-satisfied inner circle, those who held up and those who hung on, the endless stream of trivia on all levels, the stars and the burnt-out, the beautiful façade and the papier-mâché backside; there was the receptionist and the agent and Nancy and the silver-plated central figure who, one way or another, was weeping behind the flashing, well-rehearsed smile; there was the power and the glory, and there was the naïveté and the struggle for existence; and finally there were my wet trousers and those damned shoes. I wished I had the nerve to pull out my notebook and write down details, but it would be too conspicuous, and that was one thing I should by no means be. So I rehashed my impressions and stuffed them all in my memory, while thinking that my life hadn't been exactly boring, even though it had been filled with more disappointments than—than what? She would very much like to be the greatest of stars. All right, that was tangible; that was cash. I would very much like to be happy. One always wants to be what one can't explain. And one always wants to be something other than what one is. That's what separates us from the animals. So I had to be almost an animal; I was very content with myself at the moment. If I was fleeing, it was nobody's business. Who cared, anyway?

I'm breathing, I told myself into my glass.

I've got wet pants, and the shoe leather is squeezing my toes; that's pretty funny, don't you think?

But something's about to happen to you, old boy, and it may become serious.

What's serious?

Can't I imagine whatever I want?

When it comes right down to it, there's no difference between fact and fiction, is there?

There's a hell of a difference.

Drink your Scotch, and let things happen. Don't ask too many questions.

Use your body. That's what you've got it for.

I have. And it's earned me a lot of defeats and arguments, and I've been mocked because I published what I experienced.

But I did experience it.

Sure, sure.

I could easily have another refill without getting drunk.

In any case, there's nobody here who isn't drunk.

More or less.

I was ridiculed. Sometimes.

Does that embarrass you?

Nah, actually it doesn't.

Because I've got a good laugh somewhere inside me.

And smooth, warm memories of—yes, all that.

And grief.

Grief, too, admittedly.

Someone who didn't love me, whom I loved.

But you pay for everything.

Of course, that's the stipulation.

Some look like they never pay a thing.

Look like, remember that.

You can't get away from your grief and your disappointments and the mocking laughter around you. You can't get away from your body either.

I'm satisfied with it as baggage.

I'm getting a bit drunk after all.

Stop. And look at her. She's in white and silver, and beneath her dress she's naked.

She's yours—possibly.

She's a devil. Maybe. Or she's just sweet and confused and spoiled.

And not at all what they all think she is.

She'll fool you.

I'm not all that easy to fool. Despite all.

Sure you are.

I sure am not.

Suddenly, something unpleasant was happening over in the corner where she was. I heard her answer heatedly, angrily, tearfully. Then, almost running—as far as the tight dress would permit, and that wasn't much—she came over to the host and took his arm. I heard her say that she wanted to go home, now, at once, and that he, the host, had to arrange it—and they quickly left the room. She didn't look around for me, and I felt annoyed. I got up—the hell with my wet pants—and followed them out on the steps. She was standing with the host, who had beckoned a car, and the door was opened, and she got into it. I ran down the steps, noticing in a flash the surprised look of the host as I darted around the car, which was about to start, tore open the other door, and jumped in. She was sitting in the corner of the back seat, all hunched up, crying. She didn't even look at me—acted as if I weren't there. What a shrew, I thought as I pushed the shoes off my aching feet. I took out my wet, lipstick-red handkerchief and handed it to her.

"What mischief have you been up to now?" I asked.

She took the handkerchief and dried her cheeks, and her makeup was no longer fit for shooting a film. She blew her nose and sniffled.

"Well, you can tell me all about it if you want, or you can forget it. Whatever you tell me or don't tell me, I'll think the same of you," I said.

She didn't answer.

"Well, it's a deal, isn't it?"

"Shut up," she said.

I shut up—all the long way back over the Charleston-dancing turnpikes and a bridge into Manhattan—until I leaned forward to the tin soldier driving the car and gave him the name and address of my hotel. We stopped in front of it. As I had my hand on the door, she finally turned her face toward me, took my hand, and said:

"G-good-bye, I'm s-so s-sorry, f-forgive me."

"That's all right. Good-bye, sweet girl. You know where I live."

The car pulled quickly away from the curb, away with her pale face. She didn't turn around to look at me. She just sat there biting my handkerchief.

What do you know—Marilyn Monroe stuttered! That was a well-kept secret. One of many, obviously. I shook my head and stood there in my bare toes, shoes in hand, between the trash cans and the constantly flying paper on Second Avenue and rattled the locked hotel door. How delighted the desk clerk would be to see me! I rang the night bell. No one answered. I rang again, and then he came around the counter in a robe, his face very pale. He peered at me through the glass door and his face darkened when he saw who it was.

"It's three o'clock in the morning, sir. Even though America is twenty years ahead of Europe, we actually still sleep in this country."

"There are, actually, a good many people who don't, but I'm very sorry I had to wake you up."

"You think I can fall asleep again on apologies?"

"Yes, if they're humble enough. I'm really very sorry. Tomorrow I'll buy a bottle of Scotch and share it with you. You do drink Scotch, don't you?"

"Hm. It happens."

"Good, shall we let it happen tomorrow?"

"As you like, sir. Are you sober enough to help yourself to the key?"

"Oh, yes, much more so than I'll be tomorrow."

"Good Lord, you get drunk from half a bottle? I

always said it: those Europeans are real crocks."

"I'll buy two, then."

"If you insist on throwing away your money, it's fine with me."

"Thank you. You are a magnificent, generous human being. You are, actually, the best night porter I've ever met. Good night."

While I was waiting for the elevator I heard the desk clerk stomp back into the little office behind the counter and throw himself into bed with a good, solid, melodious oath:

"Up yours!"

I fell asleep, but an hour later I was awakened by the telephone.

It was the desk clerk.

"Tomorrow I'll ask the owner to throw you out."

"But I thought we had agreed to drown our sorrows together tomorrow."

"I've been awakened again, sir."

"Not by me."

"By one of your unbaptized ladies—the one with the floozy voice. She absolutely must talk to you, she says. Tell me, are you some kind of pimp, too?"

"Though I don't care to admit it, I'm neither a spiritualist, a whorehouse client, nor a pimp. But I do like Scotch."

"I've smelled that, sir."

"If I were you, I would consider it one of my more human qualities."

"Not enough for me to recommend you to the immigration authorities. You're liable to ruin a whole hotel. Shall I really put the broad through?"

"Yes, please. Actually, you couldn't do me a bigger favor."

"Darling, I'm terribly sorry I was mean to you; can

you forgive me? I'll tell you what it was that happened. I can't sleep. Won't you come over? Now?"

"Now?"

"Yes, right away. I'll leave word with the doorman so he'll let you in."

"Fine, I'll be there."

I tiptoed out of the elevator and heard the receptionist snoring. Very carefully, I left the key in its place and managed to open the glass door and get out of the hotel. I ran down the avenue, found a taxi, and rode down to Fifty-seventh Street.

The big street sweepers were rolling over the avenues and behind them the water trucks. The first light of morning was coming in over the city, cool and slow, a few early risers were scurrying along the sidewalks, and here and there a rattle was heard when the iron shutters were rolled up in front of store windows.

I was shivering a bit from cold, lack of sleep, and hangover, but my nerves were all awake in joyous anticipation. Her small-girl voice repeated the words she had said, and I was filled with glorious life. An old man was rummaging with an iron pipe in a trash can, and I was grateful that I was still young.

When the taxi turned the corner of Fifty-seventh Street, I felt as I had a few years earlier, when I took the last few steps to the summit during a mountain climb.

The doorman was standing behind the double glass door. He looked at me, let me in, and greeted me without saying anything. It was very quiet inside. I rode up in the elevator, stepped out on her floor, and saw the door ajar. I went inside and closed it carefully behind me, and she came to me in a white robe and kissed me and took my hand and led me into a bedroom with tightly drawn curtains and a very big unmade bed. She left the door ajar, so a streak of light came in from the living room, and she took off her robe and was naked and hurried into bed, pulling the quilt over herself. I undressed and lay down close to her. We held each other tightly, and she said, commanded:

"Love me, long and tenderly."

11th Day

The light of morning was already penetrating the curtains, blending with the light that came through the crack in the door, when she finally fell asleep. Not because she was sated with love, but because I had fondled her with my hands: up over her back, about her shoulders, around her neck, and up to her scalp. She lay with her back toward me, her arms stretched above her head, and her breasts, which were big and soft and heavy, swelled under my hands as they had when I made love to her. And while I was rubbing her tense body with my hands, she mumbled:

"Your hands. I knew that about your hands; they have healing powers, you know that? You caress me to sleep with your hands. Touch me; keep on touching me. Your hands have known me before . . ."

I got out of bed cautiously, put on my clothes, tore a leaf out of my notebook, and wrote:

"My darling little love: I am going now because I don't want to be in Nancy's way, but I take my happiness with me out to the streets as I walk home, and no wind will be able to blow it away from me."

I put the note on her night table amid ten containers of pills; some had tipped over. I looked at her face once more; it was quiet and peaceful. She looked as if she were about to awaken from a pleasant dream. The beginning of a smile was on her lips, but it was going through an eternity, for her sleep, having finally come, was deep; she was far, far away, in a trance. That was the way she was: far away and yet near, sleeping at the door of eternity and just about to awake—awake and smile at those who hoped for her smile. But her soul (what other word can be substituted? Damned romanticism!)—her consciousness would see even before her eyes which, when opened, found their bearings in a fraction of a second and knew what was demanded of her. That's the way you are, little watchdog, sleep well!

I closed the door, put out the light in the living room and the entrance hall, and tiptoed out, putting my shoes on outside the door. I rode the elevator down, and the doorman didn't bat an eye but acknowledged me silently and opened the door for me out into the busy New York morning. People went by, some fresh and in good form with briefcases under their arms, some shuffling along in slippers with a huge bundle of newspapers, still others just walking, and one in pajamas with a bag of fresh bread in his hand; there were also shopkeepers polishing and placing merchandise in their display windows. There was the smell of eggs and bacon and toasted bread, the first exhaust fumes from cars, a waft of beer, and a whiff of garden, and there was a police car with screeching sirens, a newspaper boy with enormous stacks of *The New York Times,* a window cleaner, and finally my best friend, the receptionist, who was wiping the counter, emptying a wastebasket, and scratching his back.

"Young man, you're actually—I mean—you shouldn't get mixed up with that sort of ladies."

"First of all, I'm not as young as I look. And *actually,* the lady is lovely."

"Sir, not with that voice. Did you get her christened?"

"She was already christened."

"O-oh! Dare I ask what her name might be?"

"Marilyn Monroe."

"Bah!"

He took the telephone receiver and wiped the mouthpiece with his big, broad, swablike finger, and everything was clean and good.

"You probably drank the two bottles yourself?"

"Not yet. I'll see you."

"Not before you've slept it off. If Miss Monroe calls, I'll say I'm sorry but the Duke of Seven-Wonder-Warner is asleep. Good day, sir."

I woke up late in the afternoon and stretched myself; I was very thirsty and felt splendid. At my bedside was a plastic bag with canned beer, which I had been provident enough to buy on my way home. I always slept naked. I sat up in bed and looked down over my body. It was scarred. I had done a good deal of what was considered foolish—just for the sake of the experience. Actually, I had also done some of it because I thought I believed in it. So what? But this morning, when I went to bed, I had taken the backpack of my past and thrown it out the window. This was here and now. Here and now. I opened one of the beers but was too lazy to get out of bed for a glass, so I drank it from the can; it tasted of metal. My hands remembered her breasts, her shoulders, her delicate neck, and her little head, her

hips that followed me as when we were dancing together, the sounds she concealed by biting a pillow, and
her skin—most of all her skin, the softest I had ever
touched, as if she were dressed in a body-stocking. I
sniffed my hands, and her fragrance was still on them,
and I stretched, feeling my vigor and strength resurge.
The body, the body. There's plenty of explanations and
excuses for him who . . . As Fred expressed it: You can
do anything if you only do it.

"There are men," I said out loud to New York. "And
there are women."

I emptied the beer can and added:

"And it's no doubt shamelessly primitive."

Then the phone rang.

The desk clerk said: "I assume you're about to wake
up, sir."

"Precisely, and now I'll run down and buy the two
bottles."

"That would be fine, sir, but unfortunately Miss
Monroe is here, and she says she wants to TALK to
you. We don't ordinarily care for ladies in the rooms."

"Good Lord, it's the middle of the day. That is the
time to TALK together."

The desk clerk faded out, and I heard her voice in the
background; then the receiver was hung up. I had the
bad habit of leaving my key in the door on the outside,
although there was a reminder on the wall always to
lock the door and never to let anybody unknown in.

Before I had time to make myself even a bit presentable, she entered with the key in her hand, closed and
locked the door, and went over to the window and drew
the curtains more tightly over it. She had actually not
come to TALK. She crept into bed with me and took
my hands and kissed them, up over my fingers to the
heel and into the hollow of the hand, just as her thumb

had done the day before; it was like stretching a hand out into a warm summer rain, feeling the drops run warmly over the skin. And she pulled off the blanket and kissed my body and snuggled up to me as closely as she could and whispered: "You were sweet to me yesterday, you weren't angry, you were sweet and good. Your hands made me sleep."

Later she sat up, crawled over to the foot of the bed, sat there naked in all the womanliness of her soft breasts, her face beaming with youth and her hair like a haycock, and asked:

"You have any champagne?"

"No."

"Scotch, then?"

"Not that either. Beer."

"Can't you tell the desk clerk to bring Scotch and soda and ice?"

"That's the one thing I can't ask him for—but that's a long story. But I'll get it from the store."

She got out of bed naked.

"I'll go with you."

"No, you'll stay. If the clerk . . ."

"How could you tell him who I was?"

"To him, the only sure thing in this world is that you're not Miss Marilyn Monroe."

"What is it with you and that clerk?"

"He thinks I'm a pimp and that you're one of my broads. Even though he knows very well that it isn't so."

"Maybe he's a bit crazy, just like you?"

"Right, honey, quite correct."

I got three bottles in a plastic bag and soda in another, and when I returned I put two of the bottles on the counter.

"You're busy, sir," said the desk clerk.

"You don't make a film with Miss Monroe in just one afternoon."

"There's a mental hospital right here in the neighborhood," he said.

"My dear friend—and you're actually the best one I have in New York—write down the number; we'll both have use for it when we've finished these two bottles."

"You think I haven't tasted Scotch before? Two bottles, phooey! If any of those ladies you haven't had the time to baptize yet should call, shall I tell them you're busy shooting a film?"

"That's fine. How would you like a part as a stunt man?"

"Always ready to serve, sir."

He swept the bottles underneath the counter and turned around to leaf through some pieces of paper.

"Once," he said, "this was a respectable hotel."

When I got upstairs, she was standing there naked, with her back turned, peering out between the Venetian blinds. She had a deep swayed cleft in her back, and her bottom was high and firm.

I took out the bottle and put it on the floor at the foot of the bed. She turned around.

"Shall we drink and TALK, or . . ."

"Do you have to be late anywhere today?"

"Mnn-no. I have to be somewhere tomorrow morning, but I can't remember where."

I gave her one of the bathroom glasses and poured, put the rest of the soda by the Scotch on the floor, and sat down at the head of the bed; she was at the foot end.

"About last night," she said. "It was one of those cynics from Fox. He once wanted to get me into bed, but I wouldn't let him; he was out for revenge. He said I made a mockery of everything serious, even my own mother. He said I was completely unscrupulous in my

73

dealings with truth as long as I got publicity, that I
didn't give a hoot about my mother, and that it was a
lie I'd done anything at all for her. I told you I hadn't
told the truth about her to begin with. But they made
me do it. It sounded good that I was an orphan. But
then somebody discovered that my mother—her name
is Gladys Baker Mortensen—was alive in a sanatorium
for—well, you know—the mentally ill. I visit her and
pay everything for her, but she can't even remember she
was married to my father. She says her name is just
Gladys Baker. She can't remember anything and
doesn't say anything, except once in a while that I'd
better stick to my modeling and stay away from the
movies because they're too unreliable. And when I take
her back to the sanatorium she's already forgotten
we've been together. You don't know how sad it is. She
was a lovely girl once, full of life and good at her job;
she was a film cutter with Consolidated Laboratories,
and there were lots of men who liked her, but at that
time . . . Maybe it all went to pieces for her because she
was ashamed that her husband left her and I was born
after he'd disappeared. She couldn't keep me, but she's
forgotten that, forgotten everything. I'm just as much
of a stranger to her as any nurse. What do they want
me to do? I have taken her out of the sanatorium when
I've been able to and tried to make her remember but
she can't; she just keeps silent. And then that bastard
says I don't care about her. I look like my mother; I'm
afraid I'll go crazy like her. My grandmother went
crazy, too, and had to be committed. She once tried to
choke me with a pillow. I know I've lied, but I couldn't
cope with them; they tempted me, and I didn't understand the consequences. And when I tell the truth, they
say I'm a cynic. I am, too, but not *that* much; anyway,
I'm not as cynical as they are. Those who are attacking

me now are the very same as made me lie then. It was one of them yesterday. You know I sometimes want to die? Even though I'm afraid of it, just the way I'm afraid of getting old. But sometimes I'd just like it to stop—the whole thing. I drink more than I ought to. I take pills, and I know I shouldn't and can't take it, and it could kill me. But I can't sleep. There are so many reasons, more than I ever could tell you, even if we talked for a whole month nonstop. And those reasons are inside my head—all of them at the same time; that's why I can't concentrate. There are psychiatrists who tell me that people have inhibitions, just like curtains that go down on the stage when the play is over, but that I don't have them, the stage in my brain is always open. I'm always thinking of a thousand other things, even in the middle of the most demanding situations. I suffer from—what is it they call it? Oh yes, tachyphrenia; it's an illness. I look very healthy but I'm not. I'm often very dizzy, and I can't hear with my right ear; it's Ménière's syndrome, and it's incurable, so I live with it and hide it and act as if nothing were wrong."

She reached down for the bottle and poured her glass full, with very little soda.

"There's also something wrong with my lower parts. I can't have children. It goes wrong all the time, and they probe, and they cut me up, and it doesn't help. So sometimes I begin to think I'm just one huge lie, all of me—that I'm born to be one. I lie to the whole world; I stand for everything I'm not . . . When I was playing *The Prince and the Showgirl,* Olivier once said to me in the studio: "Couldn't you try to be a bit sexy?" What the hell! Not even that. Tell me, there's one thing I've never asked any man, but I can talk to you; there's hardly anybody I've been able to talk to this way; tell me . . ."

75

Her glass was empty; mine, too. We had a refill. We smiled to one another, and the noise from the traffic outside turned into the kind of stillness that is the wordlessness of speed.

She bent forward a little; she was bashful in her happy nakedness:

"Tell me, am I good in bed?"

"Yes."

"Why?"

"There are about two billion women in the world. Not two of them are alike in the act of love. There are no rules. You've been married to four men, you say, and then, I assume, there are all the others. Were there any two of them alike?"

"No."

"You felt some were good and others not. Do you know why?"

"No."

"Nobody can define when a work of art is good or bad either. Some think it's good, others not. There are no rules in that case either. Some men will say about a woman that she was good, others will say about the same woman that she was not. It depends on what you expect, what you want, who you are yourself. If you could put all the people in the world into a machine and test them for all kinds of shadings and nuances, you could put together those who fitted each other best. But we always choose on the basis of chance. It's a question of luck."

"But what if I myself feel I'm not good enough?"

"Did you feel that yesterday and today?"

"No."

"There, you see."

"I once went to bed with a famous—well, one who was good, I don't want to tell you who. He wanted

76

something I didn't understand; I tried but I couldn't, and after that I've always thought I really wasn't good enough."

"You make the mistake of demanding that everything always be successful. At the same time, you know that's impossible. He didn't suit you, and you didn't suit him. Do you know Hebrew?"

"No."

"Well, there are people who can speak very well in that language. Most of us don't understand it. There is the language, there are those who speak it, and us who don't. Does that make any of us inferior?"

"No."

"Good, so don't think any more about it."

"But that's what I can't. I can't forget anything. It's all there, all the time. That's why I think I'll end up going as crazy as my mother and her mother. And that's also why I can't remember my lines. It's also because I can't sleep and take sleeping pills and can't sleep them off. But the most important is that I can't lower that safety curtain once the play is over."

"Last night in the car you stuttered. Did you know?"

"Mnn . . . yes."

"I never heard about that. Do you often?"

"It may happen all of a sudden, but it's very rare; there aren't many who know. There are men I've been married to and don't know. But I'll tell you. I'd like to tell you anything you want to know. Just ask. I've always fallen in love with men I could talk to—about myself! They listen to begin with, but then they ask me to shut up; they've heard it all. But they haven't. Because they don't give me a chance to tell the end of it —the most difficult part; I need a preliminary run for that, lots of preliminary runs. And when I notice I'm beginning to bore them, I go. I don't want to be left. I want to go myself. Now you're thinking: How dumb! Aren't you? How superficial! How damn smug! I know I'm dumb, but still I'm not. I know about films; I know more than anybody else about them. But they only discover that when the shooting is over and the film is ready. Until then, they have no confidence in what I'm doing. Because they don't know what I do—about the umbilical cord between the acting and what you see on the screen afterward. But I'm never in any doubt myself. I know exactly how every single movement is going to look once it's been filmed. That's my talent. And I have it; I know it. But Olivier didn't believe it. There are a lot of others who didn't either."

"What is it that makes you stutter—the few times you say you do?"

The glasses were empty; we filled them again. We enjoyed it and laughed at it. The world could go jump in the lake. There wasn't any tomorrow. We were finding our way to the mind behind the mind behind the mind, and we wouldn't hate each other for what we'd find and spoil everything that way. There wasn't any jealousy, any property rights, any pride that could be hurt, any vanity between us. There wasn't anything before, and what came after didn't matter right at the moment. We were just here and now—a little bit drunk, but we didn't feel that. On the contrary, we felt our brains were clear as never before. And in a way they were, too.

"There's a place in Greek mythology called Limbo. It's the place midway between life and death, where you could see everything—all you had lived, why you did it, and how you were going to be judged: to grace or perdition."

"You mean we're in Limbo now?"

"Exactly."

"And there's no telephone you can pick up afterward to call back to life and tell what you learned?"

"No, mythology has no telephones. Don't be so suspicious."

"Forgive me, but I never quite believe anybody. Why don't I?"

"Because you undoubtedly overstep the bounds of silence yourself. People always suspect others of what they do themselves."

"But I wouldn't mind if you wrote about me sometime. You're welcome to tell it all sometime. But not until after I'm dead."

"The *whole* story? Everything?"

"Yes, everything; I'll risk it. If you write it truthfully, they won't say I was a beast, even though I have been sometimes. I was raped when I was nine. Somebody wrote about it before but got it wrong. I didn't stutter as a child; it first happened after that incident. I wasn't really raped, but he forced me to do something, and I had a shock; I've never gotten over it, and it may pop up suddenly. He forced me to take him in my mouth; *that*'s the truth about it. I didn't know anything about that sort of thing; it was . . ."

"Enough to make you throw up. But you don't throw up anymore, do you?"

"No."

"One does get over the most incredible things . . . You know the bottle is almost empty?"

"Then you must go get another. I want to be staggering, stinking, cockeyed drunk. But then I won't want to screw. I don't when I'm drunk. But I do fall asleep—really fall asleep."

"There'll be a day after this one, so I'll go get another."

When I returned, she had fallen forward in the bed

and was asleep, all hunched up. I pulled her up and stretched her out, rolled her over on her stomach, and put the pillow under her head so she could breathe. She mumbled something unintelligible but didn't wake up. I wasn't feeling too good myself. On the street outside I tried to walk in a straight line but it was a difficult tightrope, although it took me in the right direction. Every once in a while I had to stop and take a deep breath, so that the skyscrapers would stop moving in on me, and before I went into the store I stood outside the window and rehearsed the items I was about to ask for. But my tongue wasn't nearly as precise as my mind, which was in a terrific state. Well, many foreigners talked funny.

"I s-should like to have a quart quart of milk, and juice, yes, also a quart, and some ham sandwicheees and s-some tea bags, and that's all . . . No, well, actually I also want a bottle of whiskey, Scotch, yes, exactly; I almost forg-got that. See how easy it is to forget things? And I guess I should also have a few bottles of soda, yes, thank you."

They directed me down the street to the liquor store for my Scotch.

All this filled an enormous bag, and I could hardly carry it, and when the desk clerk saw it, he said:

"If you've been packing, sir, you're going the wrong way!"

"They're j-just souvenirs I want to take home with me."

"So remember to take the souvenir you've got up-stairs in your room, sir!"

"You can rest quite easy. That's something n-no one will forget, and she's so small she could probably fit into a b-bag like this."

"God help the States," sighed the receptionist.

I lay down beside her but had quite a time making the room stop playing merry-go-round; then I could close my eyes, which was a big step in the right direction, and at the moment I fell asleep I was thinking it was really unbelievable how provident I always was.

12th Day

I woke up, and it was night. I looked at my watch; it was two o'clock. She was still sleeping in the same position as I had put her; it would have been a sin to wake her. So I crept into the bathroom, shaved and tidied myself up, tiptoed back, and opened the bag I had filled in the store, rediscovering my prescience. Besides sandwiches and tea there was a can of juice, and I thought it was unbelievable, but I could now remember that I'd thought of it the previous afternoon when I had seen her gulping down juice and felt we really were brilliantly suited to each other. I felt glorious . . . Then she woke up, looked around a bit confused in the half-darkness, discovered me, laughed, and stretched herself, saying:

"I'm not drunk anymore! What time is it?"

"It's exactly what it usually is when we meet: a bit past two."

"I'm thirsty," she said. "And hungry. What are you going to do about it?"

I opened the cupboard kitchenette; the light went on automatically, and I showed her the bread and tea and switched on the hot plate.

"You're wonderful, really wonderful; we should go camping together. I haven't gone camping for—I don't even remember how many years. Can't we just stay here, locked in, for a long time?"

"What about the meeting you're supposed to be late to tomorrow?"

"I'll call Nancy and tell her I've disappeared."

"And you don't think she knows where you are?"

"No. Or maybe yes. But she'd never tell. And you've got juice, too. Darling, it's either love or second sight."

"A little bit of both—or lots of both—whichever you desire, miss. We only live once."

"And what about the moral scruples?"

"We'll get to them later."

"You've got things in order, haven't you?"

She stepped out of bed, found her shoulder bag on the floor, and disappeared into the bathroom. I could hear her splashing and humming. In the meantime, I set a table on the bed, with everything the heart could desire. My hangover was a mere faint tickle in my body, a bit of a lazy good form, a solid thirst in a dry mouth, a glorious indifference to time, dates, and appointments, and the night was long, and the day . . . ? It was full of unknown opportunities. My existence didn't stretch any further than that. But it was enough. The girl in the bathtub was lovely, and it was all a bit incredible, but it was happening all the same, and isn't that what it's really all about?

She came out of the bathroom naked as she had gone in, smelling of cleanliness and sweet perfume, her hair brushed and her lips freshly colored. She sat down, wrapped the sheet around her like a sari, and took the

83

warm glass of tea in both hands. She gulped it down shamelessly and then the juice, started the sandwich, tearing off large bites and munching energetically like a squirrel gnawing a big, new, nice, fresh nut.

"There are trees all around us," I said. "And there are boulders outside the window looking like cliffs. We're camping. But it has the advantage that there are no flies and no mosquitoes. What else could you wish for?"

"You like trees, huh?"

"Yes."

"I often go up to Central Park and sit down on a bench and look at them."

"And the birds."

"I guess I've told you everything."

"Yes, almost."

"So it's your turn. Who are you?"

"I'm just a couple of years older than you are. That makes me think I'm not old enough to cope with you."

"Nonsense. I've known some younger than myself. It wasn't bad at all."

"But it didn't last."

"Nothing ever lasts. How was your childhood?"

"Outwardly, in the material sense and all that, it was splendid. But I didn't get along with my mother."

"That's too bad; that's the worst thing that can happen to you. Doesn't that make you sad?"

"Maybe. But my sadness disappeared in rebelliousness. I can't stand dictatorship in any form."

"Oh God," she sighed.

"So when the war came, I resisted—if I may put it that way, and I guess I may—and was thrown in the can, and while I was in a cell for six months I had a good long time to think things over."

"And then you wrote novels—about that?"

"Yes, about that, too."

"But you've mentioned Africa? Why did you go to Africa?"

"To get experience and to settle some accounts in my life."

"And did you?"

"No. To quote Miss Monroe: There are lots of misfits in this world. But I manage. Sometimes even quite enjoyably."

"Didn't we decide yesterday that you'd go get some more Scotch?"

The tea had been drunk, the juice and the sandwiches finished. The faint light from the cupboard kitchenette filled the room with a mild glow, as if the light came from far away—from the other side of the darkness outside the window. She extricated herself from the sheet, and her nakedness was velvety.

"I think we should do everything we did yesterday exactly like yesterday, in the same order . . ."

"Obviously, we've both got things in order."

"Sssh!"

My hands found her—an arm here, a shoulder there, a breast, a chin, a hip, a knee—and put her together in a whole figure like an artist who, lump by lump of clay, goes on to make an Aphrodite.

"I haven't been so happy in a long, long time," she whispered. "None of the ones who are trying to 'save' me would believe that."

"Sssh!"

Later she sat up naked at the foot of the bed, exactly where she had sat the day before, leaned out of bed and groped about the floor, found her glass, and held it out.

"Scotch, Mr. Lovelove!"

I poured for both of us; we drank and sat for a

moment looking at each other. Then she doubled up, smiled, and said:

"We've already got some rules to live by. They seem to work. We should never do anything else."

"As you wish. We'll never do anything else."

"You don't know how many there are who would spoil it for us if they knew what was going on."

"Will they know?"

"Sometimes I've succeeded in fooling them, but it's harder than you think. We agree that we should keep our mouths absolutely shut, don't we?"

"We agree."

"When you grow old, I think you'll come to look like President Lincoln."

"My chances of becoming president aren't very likely though."

"That's got something to do with the Constitution, doesn't it?"

"One must be born in the United States."

"I'd like to be married to the President. That would serve them right."

"Then you will."

"You think so?"

"No. But it's a fine thought."

"Then they'd stop saying I was a sex bomb."

"Does that embarrass you?"

"Yes. And I'm not, and I don't want to be. I would like very much to act in the theater. Be on the stage! Are you laughing at me even though you're not laughing?"

"No. You've got a greater talent than most people suspect."

"I've worked at the Actors Studio. Lee Strasberg says the same thing. But the strange thing—the sad thing—is that my body gets older while I don't, I mean—you understand? It's as if something in me will not grow up.

Sometimes I even think I'm going the other way—that I'm getting less able to manage, that I could do it better when I was younger. Of course, I know more about technique; I've come to grips with professionalism. But I should have grown inside, too; I should have become calmer, more secure, better able to see through people, better able to stand up for myself . . . I don't know, I can't explain it. It's . . . it's got something to do with fusing together more and more with oneself, only it doesn't happen. What happens is the opposite: I come apart more and more, get more insecure, more anxious, more suspicious. I've never wanted to be alone before. Now I want to. I feel alone, and I can't stand being alone, so why in heaven's name do I want to be alone? It's like sleeping. I want to sleep, but it's getting more and more difficult for me to fall asleep. When I was young, I didn't drink and didn't take pills; I was happier, I slept, I believed what people told me. Now I drink and stuff myself with pills, and the whole thing only gets worse, and I think more and more often of my mother and what happened to her . . . Could I have an insanity in me that grows with age?"

"No."

"How can you say that with such certainty?"

"Because the explanation is something quite different. The movies in which you have acted and will act place greater and greater artistic demands on you. The requirements grow. And your films have been getting better all the time. The latest is always better than the one before. So you're coping with it. But it's getting more difficult."

"Sometimes I'd very much like to quit—just quit completely."

"All actors want to from time to time. But they don't. They can't live without the excitement. Those who have tried have gone to pieces quicker in retirement than in the struggle on the stage. The way I figure it, the same goes for you."

"But it's so difficult. Maybe I'm too weak to make it —any of it, no matter what I choose. It looks as if I'm going from one victory to another, but I can just as easily make it look as if I'm going from defeat to defeat; I can persuade myself equally well of both. So what on earth am I supposed to do?"

"Believe in those who say you can. That you can be better. That you will succeed."

"That's what I've done. But then I begin to feel that they've persuaded me to be something else than I am —as if they'd made me invisible, I mean that part of me that's myself. I'd like very much to please everybody; much too much. I'm so impossible that even though I know it, I still do it. Don't you think I've rebelled against it? I have. But it doesn't help. Give me another Scotch, dammit!"

"It doesn't add up. If you hadn't rebelled, as you say, you'd never have been allowed to make as strong an impression in your latest films as you did. They're yours; they're all yours. You even get the directors to do what you want. There aren't many actors who've had the forcefulness to do that. You're strong enough, believe me. And if your doubt didn't grow with your contributions, you'd be exactly the dumb blonde you hate—and who you aren't."

"Oh, it sounds very good, but you know, during the past years I've noticed that I've lost energy, as if it oozed out of me. You don't know how much energy I used to have. Lots. I was strong then; I'm not anymore. Sometimes I think I'll die soon because life . . . just drips out of me like—well, I'll say it—like my monthly bleedings."

"You don't think you're the only person in the world who feels that?"

"I'm not?"

"No."

"But if that's true, how do I get over it?"

"By finding love—a man you can live with so that your career and your private life can be joined."

"Oh God, you can't say I haven't tried. I wish I could find someone I'm equal to, so we could help each other —not as teacher and pupil, not as admirer and star, but equals . . . It works to begin with, but it always ends wrong—and if it's my fault, I don't know why. The others have never been in any doubt that it was my fault when it didn't work out. There must be something very wrong with me, and the worst of it is that I don't have an inkling what it is. You haven't been so successful either, you say, and still you're giving me advice. So how can your advice be worth anything?"

"The fact that I haven't managed to live as I think I should have doesn't necessarily mean that I'm all wrong when I talk about somebody else."

"Well, I'll buy that. But even if I wanted to try again for the I-don't-know-which time, I would scare people away—the right ones, I mean . . . Would you dare? It's as if I weren't a person like everybody else. Although I hate to be looked on that way."

"But like it very much sometimes?"

"All right, yes. But I hate it more than I like it. You didn't answer my question."

"We're *not* equals."

"We could be."

"Hardly."

"There you see. It's hopeless. Even though you LIKE me with capital letters."

"Yes, undeniably."

"We go to bed together, and we enjoy it, but as soon as we let go of each other you step back from me, create a distance. Why? Do you think sometimes that I'm a slut?"

"No."

"There are lots of people who would tell you I was. But I'm not. Not in the usual sense of the word. I've slept with too many, I know it. But when I say I only did it when I was in love with them, it's true. When I was still very poor and unknown, I could have married someone rich who was a powerful man in Hollywood. He was a good man. I was incredibly fond of him. But I didn't love him, so I didn't marry him. I'm not telling you this in order to play the saint. That's just how I am. Do you believe me?"

"Yes. You're very honest."

"Oh, thank you. *Thank* you."

Tears came into her eyes.

"That's the nicest thing you've said so far."

"And do you believe that I mean it?"

"Yes."

"That's even better. Come on, there's more Scotch in the bottle!"

"We'll get drunk again."

"Nobody was ever any worse for that."

"There are indications that we're in love with each other, aren't there?"

"Absolutely."

"What are you going to do about it?"

"I'll drink with you, talk with you, touch you, go to bed with you, sleep with you, and otherwise just let things happen. How it will end, who knows . . ."

"You're right, there aren't any two men alike. Even though I once knew someone I felt almost the same way about—but not quite. No one knows about that affair;

we managed to keep it a secret. We had to. I think I could have lived with him very well, but because we had to be so circumspect all the time we finally felt like we were locked in some prison cell, and then it was ruined. I've got to keep this one absolutely secret, too. That may ruin it for us."

"Today is enough for me. In a week or two or three, or in a few months, everything may be different."

"And we won't be hurt, neither of us?"

"Not hurt enough so that we won't heal."

"Are you always so optimistic?"

"Yes, I guess so. I want to survive."

She rose and stepped out of bed, went over to the window, where I had seen her stand once before, opened the slats of the Venetian blinds, and peeked out into the night. Her beauty is of two kinds, I thought. There is the dressed one, when she is the prima donna; then she is superterrestrial. And there is the naked one, when she is a darling, sweet, amusing girl; it will take an enormously strong will to make the two of them fuse into one human being. Until they do, though, she'll probably never be happy. But I didn't want to tell this to her, even though she suspected it without accepting it. No one had yet had the will or the strength it took; that was the tragedy.

She came back and sat down on the bed. I thought: She's happiest when she's naked. That's one of the things she wanted to tell the world. But that would, of course, be misunderstood. Naked she discovered whatever was most genuine in herself. Her nakedness was the clothing in which she felt best, not because she was naked but because she was herself.

"It's strange," she said, "I can hardly remember anything from my first marriage. I was married just after I turned sixteen. I can't even talk about it coherently.

I can only remember some separate scenes. His name was Jim Dougherty. He was very sweet, and I was quite impossible as a housewife. It wasn't love. It was to get a place of my own. But I was mad about him in such a hopelessly immature way that if he should ever tell anyone about it, he would say that I was a confused little girl with a head full of foolish movie dreams, and that I was trite and silly, and that it would have been much better for me to stay a housewife and have children and lead an ordinary life. But he's wrong about that. I *wanted* to be an actress; I've always wanted that —as far back as I can remember. I was always daydreaming.

"He joined the marines. He was jealous, and I discovered that I could have whomever I wanted. I discovered the power of sex—at a distance. But I wasn't sexy— some still don't think I am!—I told you—and actually that's true; it's something I've been made to be. And I wanted to be. But deep down it's not me. It sounds incredible—depressing, wrong—not to be able to remember a marriage that lasted a couple of years. But Mrs. Dougherty was a different person; it was Norma Jean, which was my name then. You say that any one person is many people. Norma Jean is still alive inside me but in quite a different way. The Norma Jean I remember was the poor, always-hungry kid of the foster homes and the orphanage and later the one who would hang around in the agents' offices every day, hopelessly waiting for a job. But I don't remember Mrs. Dougherty. That's not to say anything bad about Jim—he was very good in his way—but somewhere along the line I was born again and became another of my selves; or maybe I just have a miserable memory, maybe I just don't want to remember it. I suppose the explanation is that my daydreams of a career were more important to me than being a respectable housewife who didn't gad about with the boys on the beach. I wasn't unhappy when I asked for the divorce; I was over that long before. If he had left me, I might have felt it quite differently; I might have cried about it and been hurt and kept on remembering all the details of the marriage. But it doesn't exist in *my* life; it's a part of Norma Jean's life, and that part of Norma Jean is not me anymore. My second marriage I've never told anybody about. No one knows about it, or at least almost no one, and those who do have kept silent. It only lasted four days. It was a Hollywood reporter. We were married in Mexico. He's among the ones who have been the very nicest to me. He didn't want to change me or to save me; he wanted me as I was. He should have hit me when I told him it was better for my career that I get married to Joe DiMaggio, but he just went to get some Scotch, and we drank ourselves silly and made love, and then it was over.

"My official second marriage—well, you know about that. It didn't last long. But Joe is a man of good intentions. When I was in City Hall and it was time to say yes to the ceremonial question, there was a second when I didn't know if I would say yes. I could just as easily have said no. I knew it would never work. But I didn't want to make a scandal—I, La Scandaleuse herself! Isn't that the expression? I don't want to say anything bad about Joe, even though his habits irritated me more than I can ever say. He was only interested in poker and baseball and TV. And spaghetti. He wanted me to wear dresses buttoned to the neck till I felt like I was choking, and he hated any kind of publicity and became furious if I made any. But I don't blame him anymore. He's one of the most helpful people I've ever met. He's one of those strong, silent men. He's the one who will always come when I'm in trouble, no matter how foolishly I've behaved. To know that Joe is there is like having a lifeguard. You said before that you hated any kind of dictatorship. So do I. He didn't want to play the dictator; he just couldn't help it. He is what he is, and that's not how I am. I was supposed to give in all the time and adapt myself, and I'm ready to; but there comes a time when I don't want to anymore. I felt more for him when I was divorced from him than when I married him. Can you understand that? Or does it sound too silly? I can't explain it any better. I respect him. And those I have respect for, I never forget; there aren't that many. Is there any more Scotch, because now comes the hardest part?

"I'm still married to Arthur—officially. But it's over. I think he may hope, once in a while, that it can still be salvaged. But I know it can't. You can be dumb and ignorant and unintellectual and still have a stubborn instinct. There's something in me—a third person maybe—which makes decisions for me, and they're final. Another of my personalities keeps them under wraps and plays on as if nothing had happened. But it *has* happened. And I'm such a coward that I continue to act as if I didn't know what's already been decided. I've never been so much in love with any man as I have been with Arthur, and it was probably the happiest moment in my life when I was married to him. He could give me everything I was missing. And he tried, oh God, how he tried! But he only saw his understanding of me, not myself. He saw the misunderstood, down-graded me, the talent that hadn't had its real opportunity; he saw the stupid film directors who forced me into the niche they had made up their mind to keep me in; he saw the mistakes of the producers, the bad scripts; and he saw the person in me that is the shy, used, love-seeking me—the upstart who had fought and gotten ahead with all odds against her and who had come through all the shit with a decency that had been so strong that not even the worst garbage had soiled it. And maybe he'll keep on thinking that way. Or no; he will give up, finally. He already has, but he won't admit it. He can divide himself up—part himself deliberately. You say all people are made up of many people; well, I understand I am too, but the difference between Arthur and me is that he observes the division with his keen eye and sees it, acknowledges it. I can't do that. All the people inside me are there at the same time in one big heap, and it's only by flashes that I can distinguish them from each other. I don't understand how he functions; he isn't happy the way I can be in the midst of the greatest mixup. He always accuses himself whereas I defend myself.

"One day when we were shooting *The Prince and the Showgirl* in England . . . it was dreadful, although . . . I'm sorry, it doesn't sound right for me to say it myself, but I know it's good, even though the reviewers didn't care for it. But the shooting was a pain; I've never been through anything worse. One day I happened to see Arthur's diary; it lay there open, and he had written in it something that . . . Well, I didn't like Olivier; there hasn't yet been another actor who so clearly showed me that he thought I was incompetent and untalented and impossible to work with, and the way Arthur wrote about it, you see, until then he had always defended me, but what he had written was the same as Olivier thought. I know that the marriage ended that day. I didn't know it at the time. He betrayed me for the first time. And the first time for me is the last—even though I may realize it only much later.

"This is not particularly coherent, I know, and not

very intelligent either. I can't sleep, I can't concentrate, I don't know if I'm good or bad in bed, I hate pain, I can't have children, it's hard for me to make decisions, I can't sustain loving relationships, I suffer from depressions and take too many tranquilizers, I drink, I lie, and I often wish to die, even though I'm sickly afraid of death and everything dead. I can't bear seeing an animal captured and killed, I want to live and die at the same time, I want to love and yet sacrifice everything for my career. I'm ignorant and dumb and vulgar, and I read books and read books and have teachers who I believe can make me a great actress, but I can't remember my lines. I'm a star, and nobody gets more fan mail than I do, but the film companies hate me, and there are producers who avoid me like the plague. I believe in marriage and faithfulness, and yet I go to bed with others. God help me, what a mess!"

The morning came in over the city and with it the traffic and noise from the street. Somebody was getting up in the hotel, and the water flushed through the pipes. The bottle of Scotch was empty.

"Take the blanket and put it over the window. I can't sleep if light gets in," she said.

I managed to hang it up with some safety pins, and the room became fairly dark.

Her skin was whiter than the white bed linen.

For the curious: Marilyn was not frigid as some have maintained. Nor was she a sex acrobat as most think. She was just very, very sweet. What, then, is the explanation of the Marilyn Monroe mystique? She was not what one understands as an "elegant" girl. She was not long-legged and beautiful in the classical sense. On the contrary. Her legs were too short and her thighs a bit too thick. Nor was her stomach by that time flat; it was very clearly too pudgy. Neither were her breasts as firm as those of very young well-shaped girls. She had a good figure, but so many girls do. But watching a film like Some Like It Hot *makes you realize that it's she who makes it into something more than a funny comedy. The other actors are good, and the director, Billy Wilder, has perhaps never shown better craftsmanship. The dialogue is witty, the action rich in tempo and funny ideas. And yet it would never have been anything more than good entertainment if she hadn't been there. She makes the film into a work of art about love. And even in another twenty years it will still be a film classic because she makes it vibrate with love.*

There was a dynamism in her that incessantly produced erotic vibrations so strong that they affected the camera and the roll of film and jumped out from the movie screen. They emanated from her even when she walked around in a robe, with a greasy face, or hid in the street or in a bar behind the taut kerchief she wrapped around her head, wearing big, dark glasses and unpressed pants; or when she wore an expensive lace dress; or when she waded on the beach, splashing the water up around her; or when she lay in bed or huddled up in the corner of a sofa, gazing out at something far away and indiscernible to others; or when she gushed out her life in a confusion of sentences, or was drunk or depressed or happy.

She was . . . ?
She was.

13th Day

I woke up shortly after noon. She was lying on her back beside me, her eyes open, staring up at the ceiling. Her face was pale—paler than the paleness of her skin; there were black shadows under her eyes, and her face was bloated. She looked ill.

"No, I'm not sick, not that way, I'm . . . I'm sorry, but I'm down. I haven't slept. I was just about to, when you fell asleep, but then I couldn't anyway. I have a slight hangover, too, but that's not so bad. I'm having an anxiety attack. I don't want to go out of bed, or out of the room, or outside—out to everything out there— but I have to; otherwise, things will happen that shouldn't happen. But I don't have the strength to play the game. At one point while you were so quietly asleep —you know you sleep totally silently? I couldn't even hear you breathe—I was thinking I would ask you, when you woke up, to take me away from here, far away, from everything, from America; hide me some-place where no one could find me. And I would never perform again, and you'd let me cry when I wanted to or couldn't help it, without asking me why, and afterward you'd act as if nothing had happened. And we'd find a beach where there were no people and just wade in the water, and there'd be nothing else—no yesterday, no tomorrow—and somehow you'd make me happy again, and the most important things in life would be the beach and the water and our solitude and the food we would make. And we'd love each other, and you'd write your books, and I'd read, and it would be quite silent around us. It's probably because I've thought that way about us that I'm so happy with you, even though I don't know you. How can I know that you're not like the others and have secret thoughts about taking advantage of me? That's how it's always been. At first I believe the men I fall in love with, some of whom I've married, but it always ends the same way. We quarrel, and they can't stand me, and I begin to suspect them: that they still wanted to use me, even though they always denied it and got terribly indignant when I said it. And then I'm back where I began and start wondering what to do with my next film and how best to perform the comedy that is my life. I make others believe in something I know all the time is wrong, and then I suddenly discover that I can deceive myself, too —that I can momentarily believe the vital lie I play for them—until I can't go through with it and can't sleep and take too many pills and break down and have to begin from the beginning again . . . I never get out of my own vicious circle. And then I think about my mother, locked up in a mental hospital, and that my grandmother and grandfather died insane and I'm at the verge myself . . . When I was seven, my mother bought a house in the northern part of Hollywood, near the Hollywood Bowl. I can remember it clearly, we were so happy, but it didn't last long. She rented most of the house to some Englishmen working in Hollywood. We each had our own room, mother and I, but in 1934, in January—the worst in Los Angeles; it always rains—my mother had an attack of hysteria and was tied down on a stretcher and taken to the hospital. It was frightful, even though it wasn't the first time my life fell apart. In a way I think I always expected it to end badly; anything good ends badly. And yet I had hoped . . . If I ever have a child—which I won't, I'm sure—there's one thing it should have above anything else: security. Its life should be the same day by day; it should never be afraid that what's most important could suddenly change. But then I think I can't even guarantee that, because how do I know what will happen to me? Maybe it's that way in our family, that when we reach a certain age we go mad . . . My mother has paranoid schizophrenia . . . Don't I, too? Or won't I? Can anybody guarantee that I won't? No! Right? So I'd better go on as *I* am with people forcing me to live a certain way; maybe it's all preordained? I'm crazy about going to fortune tellers, even though I know that no two of them have ever said the same thing and I feel, somewhere inside me, that what will happen to me *has* been decided—which destroys my belief that anybody can really help me, even through mutual love. But then I think I'm too self-centered and that other people have the same thoughts but are calmer and more sensible about them and can free themselves from them more easily and control themselves, and I think I could do the same if I pulled myself together. But how am I supposed to pull myself together when I can't sleep and have to begin the day sick for lack of sleep and my body aches from it and my thoughts chase each other around as if they were gamecocks—I once saw a cockfight in

Mexico, and I can't tell you how disgusting it was—and then and then and then . . . I can remember things well; there's nothing wrong with my memory, even though many times while filming I've been quite impossible and haven't been able to remember even the easiest lines. But that's for other reasons. I remember things well—better than anybody I know will believe. It really may be that I suffer from some kind of memory sickness; I'm always remembering thousands of events and sentences and people—every single moment—and each time I have to concentrate on one single thing I have to pull myself together, really make an effort to pull myself together in order to stop this crazy stream of pictures . . . I say that because I read in one Camus' books you said I should read . . . well, there's a place, when he's writing about the beauty of the Mediterranean—I've never been there, but I would like to so much—he writes that together with the beauty that emanates *from* the sea, extending to the curves of its perfect bays, there also emanates an excess of anxiety, and then he says that—I think I'm quoting him correctly: 'The tragic culminates in this sun-gilded catastrophe.' When I read that, I knew it was me."

She stood up naked and still happy in the dress of her nakedness. She took a look into the plastic bag I had brought the night before.

"I guess there's no more juice?"

"No, but I'll run down for more."

"Thank you, you're always sweet to me. But listen, I have to leave you now, and please don't come looking for me, and please don't tell anybody we've been to-gether—nobody at all. You promise? I'll try to come back—maybe in a few days, maybe in a week, maybe in two weeks; I don't know. It depends. I have to lie a lot, but I have a plan; maybe it can work out. I don't know, but I promise you I'll try. I've been so happy these days; I'd like to be again . . ."

I dressed hurriedly, kissed her, and went for more juice.

When I was leaving, she called out to me: "I'm crazy about hot dogs, too!"

The desk clerk looked with a care-worn expression at the plastic bag I had with me when I returned. I went over to him, opened it, and showed him the contents.

"Juice, juice, and hot dogs! I'm afraid this is becoming a respectable hotel again."

The desk clerk sighed: "I am, too!"

"But I thought . . ."

"If you're not getting drunk on Scotch, I'm afraid of what you'll think of next! By the way, shall I book you for a double room?"

"No, unfortunately; she's leaving. I'll be very lonely for the next few days."

"The hell you will! But since you're not drinking and not going to bed with Miss Monroe—will you be kind enough to warn me what I may expect next?"

"Emptying two bottles of the golden stuff with the receptionist."

"Oh, I thought you'd forgotten all about it."

"Some things should *never* be forgotten."

"Sir, that's the truest word you've said so far."

She was dressed when I came up, but had no makeup on, and the kerchief was again tautly tied around her hair. She was even more unrecognizable than when she arrived.

We sat down on the bed, drank the juice, and ate the hot dogs. She was silent for a long time.

Then she said: "While I'm away, I think you should write as many scenes of that screenplay as you can, based on your synopsis. You'll write it differently now.

Show it to Fred, while you're working on it. He knows me, and he's in a position to judge it. We haven't gotten around to talking about it. We should have, but . . ."

Suddenly she laughed that little laugh of hers, and seemed revived. She leaned forward and kissed me, got up, collected her shoulder bag, stood for a moment looking at me, waved, and was out of the door.

What was left of her was only her fragrance—that sweet body smell with a tinge of absinth in it—the dents made by her body in the quilt and the mattress, the empty juice containers, the greasy paper from the eaten hot dogs, the sound in my ears of her small, intense, searching, inquiring, testing voice.

I went into the bathroom, where she had rummaged through my toiletries to find something; everything was spread all over the sink, the bathtub, and the windowsill. Under my shaver I found a piece of paper on which she had written in her jumpy, unsure handwriting, the letters leaping like frightened animals:

Diamonds Are a Girl's Best Friend
—but what if they aren't?
Do you know the answer to that?
Anyway, thanks. Love, M.

14th Day

I had *felt the same way before. And yet it was different —quite different. It was as if I had faced a special work of art: It told me something so forceful and strong that I felt I couldn't contain it. The sheer force of it shattered and exhausted me but at the same time made me feel unbearable tension and anxiety because I couldn't live with it inside me. I had to defend myself against it, but I could not forget it. I felt myself crushed by it, and at the same time I was filled with wild happiness to have come across it. I thought: I have rediscovered life, and that is the same as understanding that life can leave me.*

15th Day

"There's a call from Hollywood," said the desk clerk. "It's Miss Monroe. She sends regards and says they won't pay more than one million dollars for the script . . . Frankly, sir, if you want my opinion, that's too bad!"

"Only one million! That's impossible. But perhaps you should let Miss Monroe . . ."

"Sir, considering all the Scotch you pour out, not to mention the juice and the tons of hot dogs . . . Well, the hell with it all; here's the broad!"

She could get away for half an hour, she said, no more, but she had good news. So, if we could meet right away, she'd like to go to Central Park; the weather was so good.

"There's an entrance to the park not far from my hotel," I said. "So if you take a taxi, I'll be waiting downstairs on the sidewalk."

I went down, looked broken-heartedly at the desk clerk, and hissed: "One million—the pigs!"

"Well, sir, some aren't worth more . . . !"

I went out in the sun, got a beer in a nearby snack bar, and sat down on a step to wait. An hour passed, but she came.

"You know what?" she said. "I'm really hungry. I haven't eaten a thing all day."

"So let's go to the snack bar."

We found an empty table, and she said she wanted eggs and bacon.

I went to the counter, and when the guy standing at the cooker turned to get my order and I had given it to him, he asked:

"You wanna 'em turned round or sunny side up?"

He said this with all of Idaho's potato crop in his mouth. I gaped, for it's a good deal more intelligible in print. I tried to explain that I hadn't understood.

"You carned get a both same time, ma-an!"

Marilyn came to my help, saying she wanted them "turned round."

The cook brought our plates, slamming them hard on the table.

"Is he deaf?" he asked her.

"He's not an American," she said.

"Thank God for that," the cook replied, and returned to his range, shaking his head.

"You just shouldn't live so far uptown," she said. "Why do you?"

"Because I like it."

"Why?"

"It's equally far from the wealth and the slum. This is where most people live."

She looked at me a while, thinking, and then said:

"It's those people who have given me my fame—"

"Right, my clever girl."

"You make me think of something. I'm doing something wrong."

"Do what you want to do. You have the opportunity."

"I almost never do what I want to do. Do you?"

"For the most part. That is, when I know what I want."

"Do you always know?"

"No, sometimes I don't—and sometimes I discover that I really didn't at all want to do what I thought I wanted to and therefore did!"

"It's difficult, isn't it?"

"Damn difficult! 'Turned round or the sunny side up'!"

We ate, and then she said we could walk for five minutes in Central Park.

Just inside the entrance a Japanese cherry tree had begun to blossom.

"Oh, that's pretty, it's so darling! I came to tell you that I think it'll work: to abscond without anybody knowing. Are you happy?"

"Everything is good and beautiful."

"You mean it's beautiful to be in love?"

"Yes, don't we both mean the same thing?"

"Yes, that's exactly it. We see the same thing without being forced to. Just think, for once!"

16th Day

I went out in an excited, sentimental mood and bought myself juice and hot dogs. Well, yes, beer, too. I tried to write but didn't succeed. I wanted to write something quite different from the film that had been planned in my synopsis. But I had no film. On the other hand, I felt this intense excitement, this happy sorrow that may be experienced when coming out of a movie theater after seeing a great film. I had nothing but a feeling— no action, no idea, no lines. I was a writer without thoughts but with a mind inebriated with love and wonder, full of the desire to write but torn by everything I had been and wanted before. I couldn't even write down what I felt, although it would have been a serviceable catalogue of my confusion. I thought of Leonardo's painting of the Archangel Gabriel, touching the human Adam with one finger. A life had been kindled in me —a wild life—but I didn't know how to live it. I felt ashamed of myself, ashamed over my happiness, ashamed to write because I was too small, too untalented, too weak to carry out the task that had been placed on me.

Finally, I gave up and went down to the desk clerk, and we retired into the little office and night quarters behind the counter and opened the first bottle of Scotch. The desk clerk told me about the time when he had been a soldier during World War II. He had been among those who crossed the Rhine. There was also Paris, the refugees, the dead—all the dead; the same story that all veterans told. But I remember that at one time or another, while we were still able to speak more or less sensibly, he said: "I don't want to offend you, sir, but Europe was shitty and decayed. New York is also shitty, admitted. But America is not decayed, you understand? I mean, there's still the dream, and part of the dream is the pride in knowing that we still have a chance to make it come true. Europe has no dream; it has despair and boasts about it. Europe puts on airs about its own ugliness, its ruins, its bad conscience. I hated being in Europe. The girls and the cheap liquor and all that, yes, sure, and I'm only a hotel desk clerk —just one of the underpaid—but we don't put on airs over the fact that we've sacrificed ourselves for your failed ideals and your ridiculous dictators; we don't even cry about it. We don't think about it anymore; it was there, and it's over, and we intend to go on. You're an egghead, sir, no offense intended; don't misunderstand me. It's a fine Scotch you bought. But I'm proud of my country. It is so strong that it can change its face overnight, and tomorrow we may do something we didn't even know we would touch the day before—if necessary. Necessity, sir, that's the name of the U.S. game: to do what's necessary. And that's not something we can be directed or forced to do. We have presidents and all that, but here it's the people who decide what's necessary. You Europeans, you come with your prejudices, you only want to see what you've already decided you want to see: gangsters and slums and, well, yes, all the things you drivel about. But you don't see the truth about us, the strength, the ability to admit a mistake and correct it, to remake the things that aren't good enough, instead of whining over our own sordidness like you do and even brag about it. I'm sorry to say it, sir, but I can't stand Europeans, though otherwise you're a fine man, sir, and the only thing I'm sorry about is this bit with the broad that looks like Miss Monroe. You mustn't misunderstand. The real Miss Monroe is fine; she's one of ours. She's a girl of the people, whatever they say, those eggheads—the hell with them—they're not true Americans. The rest of us who don't write and only see her in the movies, we're proud of her. She's one of the stars in the flag. Believe me!"

The rest is silence, not of the Shakespearean kind but the potent wordy silence that has Black Label gummed on it, and Europe and America finally went to bed with bloated heads and wobbly legs and feet that walked by themselves. I lay down on my stomach and stretched out my arms so I could grab hold of both sides of the bed in order to cling to it and myself and her.

17th Day

White paper in the typewriter. But the idea I had been so excited about—a witty, satirical comedy about a European's confrontation with all that was different in America—was now impossible. If I was to write anything at all, it had to be a new version of an American tragedy. And that, too, was impossible, not to mention presumptuous.

I didn't succeed; of course I didn't. You need peace of mind to write; that's what I had the least of. But I remember that I was burning to do it. I wanted to give the best gift an author can present: to write a text for someone he loves, so that she may become more real, more accomplished, and more beautiful as an artist than ever before; to elicit the distinctive characteristic of her talent, be her servant, obliterate himself for her sake.

But that's not what you're doing, I hear her say—here in the room of the lonely house near the sea she never got to see, which is not silent as the Mediterranean but beats its drum in an unchanging slow tempo behind the cliffs between the shore and the house. It's only now that a word is appearing on the white paper—so long afterward, when I finally feel that the age difference between us has become wide enough. That time it was only three years. And even though the three years were mine, I felt many years younger in the sense that I didn't have courage enough, not knowledge enough, and not boldness enough to dare—and therefore be able to write about her and to her. I hear her voice in this room filled with ghosts. The desk clerk is sitting heavily in the chair facing me. Somewhere in the room you are standing in the white lace dress. "But that's not what you're doing," you say.

You're right. What good would that be, anyway? Facts and alleged facts have been plowed through countless times in scores of documentary books about you. Even if I could add a couple of items, what would be the point? No one got any closer to you for that reason. It is true that you didn't engage in monologues as I have made you do, but I have no regrets about presenting them that way. As arias. They were dialogues. You spoke in short sentences. You answered questions. And many of your answers were attempts at evasion. But what you said was what I have written; only the style is different. So let's call it novelistic documentarism. I have only one wish: to find as much as I can of the truth behind what happened and what was said. But I still feel some of the anxiety I experienced so strongly that time, so many years ago ... Anxiety? Perhaps apprehension is a better word. Even though you said I should write about you when you were dead, how do I dare? Especially today, when everybody can plainly see how great you were, how you reached out of your roles, out of the film's action, its dimension, its touching romanticism, to touch every single viewer in a personal encounter.

Norman Mailer writes about you that "she was certainly more and less than the silver witch of us all. In her ambition, so Faustian, and in her ignorance of culture's dimensions, in her liberation and her tyrannical desires, her noble democratic longings intimately contradicted by the widening pool of her narcissism (where every friend and slave must bathe), we can see the magnified mirror of ourselves, our exaggerated and now all but defeated generation, yes, she ran a reconnaissance through the Fifties, and left a message for us in her death, 'Baby go boom.'"

18th Day

A day was gone, and there was still nothing on the
paper. A myriad of ideas emerged; all were scrapped.
I suspected that somewhere in my imagination the right
idea was waiting to be found. I paced the floor back and
forth, lay down on the bed and stared up at the ceiling,
peeked out of the window, out over the skyscrapers and
down at the traffic, sat down at the typewriter, gave up
again, and went down to the snack bar and had something to eat. I returned hoping that the receptionist
would tell me she had called, that there was a message;
but there was nothing, and in a way that was also the
best, for there was nothing I could suggest to her. This
little room was all there was, and it was like a gondola
tossed between the cliffs of New York with me as the
only passenger. And there was my longing for her, my
love for her, together with my sober recognition that
she was on her way—in a breathless, directionless race
—toward a future of which she herself had no clear
idea, the only driving force being ONWARD, while

voices called out to her to do this and that. But she hardly listened, for the voice she wanted to hear had to be her own, and it was the most silent of all. How foolish of me to believe that she would listen to mine, even if I could make out what I wanted to say. But she expected it, and I didn't want to disappoint her—provided I saw her again at all! The fantastic aspect of our history together didn't make it very likely that there would be more "days" with me and her. What else could this be than a fancy idea? Who had told me she fell so easily, so quickly, and impulsively in love? The psychological consequence was that it also ended easily, quickly, and impulsively. That much sense was still left in me.

But the idea finally came. It suddenly dawned on me that she had told me her story, the true story no one knew—not the public at any rate—and perhaps she wanted . . . She who had dared the big leaps, despite all warnings, and who had the ability to hear what was happening among the masses that loved her and admired her acting, to hear that mighty anonymous voice through the film directors' commands, the film czars' warnings and "good advice"—hadn't she been right? The nude calendar had not harmed her, as all her advisers had thought it would; on the contrary, it only made her more popular. She had the talent of a great leader to perceive the voice of the people while it has still not been articulated, to utilize its enormous thrust against all her opponents, and to steam-roll her way through the formidable road blocks until they broke and she could decide what she herself wanted. So why not try, if she would let me—attempt to write her story, let her play herself, revealing all, act out her own incredible life, raw, unveiled, and unadorned, and perhaps carry it closer to the hopes she had . . . She who went to fortune tellers—let her be her own fortune teller and play her dream of reaching the theater, Broadway's stage, just as her teacher, Lee Strasberg, had assured her she would be able to. Perhaps he would warn her against it, but why shouldn't he be wrong just as all the others had been? She had long ago broken out of the category in which they had stuck her, that of the dumb, blonde sex bomb, and in her latest films she had displayed her talent for dramatic acting ever more forcefully. True, it was still seen only in flashes, but it was there, and she rebelled against being the queen of the Hollywood comedy; she wanted to show them she had her own identity and she worked hard for it . . . Why shouldn't she finally succeed in being the Grushenka of *The Brothers Karamazov* that she was sure she was capable of?

Billy Wilder, who directed two of her best films, *The Seven-Year Itch* and *Some Like It Hot,* said that "God gave her everything. The first day a photographer took her picture she was a genius."

In the eulogy that Lee Strasberg delivered at her burial on Thursday, August 9, 1962, he said: "Despite the heights and brilliance she had attained on the screen, she was planning for the future; she was looking forward to participating in the many exciting things which she planned. In her eyes and in mine her career was just beginning. The dream of her talent, which she had nurtured as a child, was not a mirage. When she first came to me I was amazed at the startling sensitivity which she possessed and which had remained fresh and undimmed, struggling to express itself despite the life to which she had been subjected. Others were as physically beautiful as she was, but there was obviously something more in her, something that people saw and recognized in her performances and with which they identified. She had a luminous quality—a combination of wistfulness, radiance, yearning—to set her apart and yet made everyone wish to be part of it, to share in the childish naïveté which was at once so shy and yet so vibrant. This quality was even more evident when she was on the stage. I am truly sorry that the public who loved her did not have the opportunity to see her as we did, in many of the roles that foreshadowed what she would have become. Without a doubt she would have been one of the really great actresses on the stage." Norman Mailer ends his biography of her on these words: "And if there's a wish, pay your visit to Mr. Dickens. For he, like many another literary man, is bound to adore you, fatherless child."

None of this could be known to me as I sat, a young man, in a small room with my silent typewriter. And it is possible that even the great teacher and artist, Lee Strasberg, fell victim to the mystery that was the secret of her success, the aura of the little girl with her vital anxiety, her volatile temperament, her nervous shyness, her pendulum swings between the failing belief in herself and the immovable obstinacy that made her talents soar in a dazzling perfectionism. . . . At long last I sat down at the typewriter and began to write her story.

19th Day

There was still no word from her. But I didn't despair, for I was convinced that the intensity with which I was thinking of her as I wrote and wrote would reach her and make her think of me and suddenly appear again . . . The words kept pouring into the synopsis I was working on, all the facts I could command viewed through my new knowledge of her. I felt it was forming something that could become a film quite different from any other in which she had played. I was sure that now it would be successful and she would be enthusiastic about my idea, and I forgot all the walls and Spanish cavalry and trenches that await anybody who dares move forward to the creation of a new film.

In the evening, with muscular rheumatism in my back from writing, tired in my fingertips, and dizzy in the head, I went to the movies and saw *The Prince and the Showgirl* once more. Naturally, my experience of it was different from what it had been the first time. I heard a new sadness in her laughter, a yearning in her

dreams, a tenderness in her love. I left the theater rein-
forced in my belief that there were no limits to what she
could perform; she would not be frightened by the
openness and self-confidence that a film about her own
life would demand . . . Had any other screen actress
shown such courage, such strength, in her rebellion
against Hollywood? She had defied and overcome the
taboos of scandal. She had, even in her insecurity, stood
by her shortcomings, which she knew better than anyone else, and won the love of a world audience. She had
shown herself naked and survived it amidst envious
bigotry, for her nakedness was not that of piquancy,
effrontery, or sex worship but that of purity. Take me
or leave me, that's how I am, and no one will ever make
me be any different!

20th Day

"Hey, Hans, you look like death warmed over, you're so pale! Has it affected you that much?" said fat Fred.

I put my synopsis on his desk. It was fifty pages.

"I've been writing this for two days."

"Oh, so that's it. That makes me breathe easier."

"What else could it be?"

"Her. She's prone to falling in love, and that usually makes people terribly wacky—and pale-faced. I heard a bird singing. But don't feel obliged to initiate me into the world's most interesting love story. Quite aside from the fact that I've heard it twenty times before, you have promised her not to tell it to ANYBODY!"

"You're well informed."

"One has to be in my line of business. Did you write anything sensible?"

"Hardly. In any case, not what we had agreed on."

"Oh, God, then it *is* crazy."

"That idea we had is impossible for me now that I know her. It's too superficial, too silly. But here is a

synopsis of a film that is her own story. She's going to act her own life."

"Has she agreed to that?"

"No, I haven't had the chance to show it to her."

"She'll never go along with it."

"And why not?"

"It's premature. They'll say she'll make herself ridiculous with it. They won't put money in it. There are other reasons, too."

Fred took my manuscript, leafed through it, came to the last part, and read.

"You have her end up in the theater. You said it was her own story. She's never acted on a stage. And she never will."

"I'm sure she will."

"You don't know her. I do. And so do all the people in the business who are supposed to back the project. Nobody believes it. I thought as much; she's turned your head around. As usual. She's film, and she's the biggest in film today. Theater—that's hopeless; I assure you, I know. If anyone lets her out on a live stage, it'll kill her. If that film were made, it would be tantamount to driving her out of the movies into the theater, and then she'd be finished. It would end in scandal and breakdown and perhaps something worse. Why won't people ever stick to what they can do?"

"Because they believe and feel they can do something else and more. It doesn't have to be mere conceit so believe in oneself."

"You know that Arthur Miller is writing a film for her. He's turning the short story 'The Misfits' into a screenplay and writing a role for her into it. I haven't read it yet, but I don't think I'm wrong figuring that the role will tax her to the utmost of her performing abilities. Many of us dread the consequences. It could be her breakdown. But, all right, the attempt is exciting, so in God's name let's make it—and cross our fingers until they become crooked with rheumatism. But this . . ."

He threw my manuscript on the table.

"If you absolutely want to try to get it through, you'll have to wait, and wait long, and if you want my opinion, so long that it'll be too late. Go home, and write around the idea we agreed on. It's good enough; I have a chance to get it financed. But you probably also want the impossible?"

"When you ask like that, it's because you know the answer."

"Unfortunately, yes. But I have known people to come to their senses, though admittedly seldom. It's a pity," he said and stood up. "I think we could have worked well together."

21st Day

The next one to offer advice was, of course, Nancy. It didn't surprise me. There was an honor guard of rescuers around Marilyn who were eminently well informed. They met in the bar by the United Nations, often in the same booth. But Nancy had changed. It was as if she had shriveled, and she spoke to me in a whisper that wasn't only due to the fact that no one was supposed to hear it.

"Marilyn always gets a lot of energy when she falls in love," she said. "I've seen it so often. But it doesn't last. I know you don't believe me, so I could have saved myself the trouble of asking you to come and talk to me. But I couldn't help it. I don't know you. You look serious to me. But you could be an adventurer; what do I know? I can't do anything, I realize that. But you should know that one day you'll have a breakdown to contend with—a tragedy. I don't expect you to believe it. You've met a famous star. She's a warm and incredibly sweet girl, she's a genius, and momentarily she believes that there are undreamed-of possibilities ahead. But there is so much behind that you know nothing about. And I wish for your sake that you'll never find out. I really do, even though you'll hardly believe me. But in the end Marilyn has always decided her own fate. She's tried to adapt herself, and she's even succeeded from time to time—at least as long as she wanted to—but in the end she decides her life herself, though there are many who don't believe it. They look upon her as the eternal sacrifice, usually by the high priests who maintain that they only want what's best for her, but deep down want what's best for themselves. But that's only the beginning of the truth about her. When the ceremony draws to a close, she herself wields the knife. Not that I blame her for it; she's fighting for her *own* survival. That's only her right, just like it is anybody else's. But if you remember what I've said, there may be a hope, however small, that what is beginning as a tragedy may be reduced in the end to a mere disappointment. And that's bearable—for both parties. I can't wish you good luck, even though I'd like to!"

22nd Day

The desk clerk merely said: "The dame is here!"

I barely managed to open the refrigerator and pull out the bottle of Dom Perignon before she was there with my key, which she held aloft in her hand.

"Are you always this absentminded?"

She locked the door, took off her gangster sunglasses, threw her bag on the floor, put her hands around my neck, and kissed me.

"We'll let the champagne wait," she said. "And put the blanket up over the window!"

When I got down from the chair, having applied the safety pins, she was in bed. The mystery; the gentle, glad, tender, soft mystery. In the soft brown light, her hair flooding the pillow like white ashes, I gazed at her face and into her big eyes to find some trace of the tragedy which I thought had threatened, but I found only blue, boundless affection.

Afterward, with the filled champagne glass in her hand, she said in a quick, somewhat halting voice:

"I've arranged it so that no one will be able to find us for a week or two. I'm sure nobody will get wind of it, so you shouldn't feel sorry that I have to go again now. I'll be back tomorrow, and then we'll go. We'll drive as far as we want to, and one way or another we'll end up in Hollywood. I have to discuss my next film with Fox; Fred is there, too. And then we must see if we can fit yours into the plans. I don't know. They're pressing me, all of them, and they're forcing me with their damned contract. But let's wait and see, many things can happen . . . I can't stop thinking all the time about that quote we found—'the tragedy of the sun-gilded catastrophe.' They all want to eat of me. I'm afraid, but I'm also glad I can give them the slip, even if it's only for a little while . . . I've had a nightmare with knives cutting pieces out of me, but you'll help me, won't you? Whatever happens, will you help me?"

"I would like to love you."

"Don't you already?"

"Yes, but there's a whole army ready to prevent me from helping you."

"Darling, don't talk rubbish. Tomorrow. Be sure you've packed and checked out. Time is short."

23rd Day

We had agreed that she would arrive at noon, and even though it was clear to me that I would outdo her in naïveté if I thought she'd be punctual, I still took my one suitcase (containing a newly cleaned dinner suit) and my typewriter down to the receptionist at exactly 12 o'clock.

Good Lord, I said to myself, the lovesick must be forgiven much!

"You *are* serious, sir! When you told me yesterday, I definitely thought it was one of your fancy ideas."

"If the 'dame' shows up it's no fancy idea."

"Well, then I won't check you out because it *is* a fancy idea."

"How's that?"

"That sort of 'dame' doesn't show up—unless you're a director of 20th Century–Fox. And that you definitely are not."

"No, unfortunately."

"Why in heaven's name don't you stick to the plan

you told me about before, when we were talking sense together? Write the comedy, sir; nobody can write anything amusing anymore, and there are, God help me, enough tragedies every day. Since Steinbeck's *Tortilla Flat* nothing really funny has been done. Well, yes, the Marx Brothers."

"I still want to write a film, but it's not going to be funny."

"You mean it'll be just like all the others."

"That wasn't my intention."

"I suppose it's going to be about love, or unhappy love—which is pretty much the same anyway."

"It's going to be about a person who fights her way, against all odds, from abject poverty, orphanhood, and ignorance, to stardom. But shadows follow. The light increases, but so do the shadows. Yet, it's going to end well."

"Seems to me I've heard, seen, and read the story before."

"Most works of art are about the same; it's the style that makes the difference."

"Well, you've got a point there. But forgive me, sir, aren't you a bit conceited. I mean, you're not quite that famous, are you?"

"No, but there's always the first time."

"Actually, I never, ever imagined that I could repeat what General Patton did."

"But he did it."

"Because he was General Patton. You know, sir, actually you're one of the most sensible Europeans I've met. It's a pity it had to end this way for you. Will you be coming back here when the 'experiment' is over?"

"Yes, definitely."

"Good, then, together, we can celebrate that you've become a little wiser—whether it succeeds or not . . .

Excuse me, I have some accounts to bring up to date."

At one o'clock I told the desk clerk that if she came, I had gone out to the luncheonette on the corner for breakfast.

I sat by the window, so I could look down the sidewalk if she'd turn up. She didn't. I went over to the opposite corner and into a bar which was placed so that I could keep an eye on the hotel entrance, and started on my first Scotch.

Marilyn's good friend, Norman Rosten, who wrote a warm and beautiful book about her five years after her death, tells us that one gray afternoon when he visited her in her Manhattan apartment and saw her stand gazing out of the window that overlooked the East River, he began a poem about her:

> *You stand, finger at your lips, lost*
> *In a long-abandoned heaven . . .*

And he adds: "She lies on the couch, asleep, her head turned to one side, hair seeming to flow back upon the pillow. Her blouse is open at the throat, an artery pulses against the pale skin. Her breathing is regular, peaceful. She is a child despite the long artificial lashes, the carefully done hair, the voluptuous body; the spirit of the child hangs over her like an innocent light. Her eyelids tremble, a dream perhaps . . . ?

"Her eyes open. She answers, fully awake. 'What day is it?' "

Of the many books that have been published about her, there's hardly any that has described her more correctly. Those were just the kinds of thoughts I had, but they were first written down many years later.

She wasn't unfaithful in order to be cruel to those she

failed. She didn't arrive late to mock those who were waiting for her. She didn't get drunk to show her contempt. She never wanted to do anybody any harm. She wasn't malicious. She was never indifferent to anybody. Not to anybody. What she most wanted was to make everybody around her happy. She wanted to do her best in terms of what others expected of her, but she just couldn't do it. She didn't drink because she was a wilful drunk or even an alcoholic, but because there was something in her that was stronger than the wish to please and be adaptable. She didn't ruin her health with sleeping pills and tranquilizers because she was addicted, but because she couldn't sleep, couldn't seal off her nerves at the end of each day, couldn't berth at the moment's wharf. She didn't lie because she found pleasure in it, but because she didn't want to hurt others with her own imperfection. She didn't fall in love because it might be advantageous but because she fell in love. And she didn't leave the men she had enthralled —no one who has loved her can ever forget or cease loving her—to satisfy herself and to exchange one man for another who at the moment seemed to be more advantageous for her, but because they couldn't contain her and because she suffered from eternity's claustrophobia. She was called a star, and that's just what she was. She could only exist in an infinity that wasn't of this world. That's about how my thoughts went that warm day drawing toward evening on Second Avenue in New York, while the ups and downs of the Scotch tested the agility of my intellect.

Then she came—in a white, open Buick Skylark convertible. Out of it stepped a fantastic lady. She was wearing striped slacks that looked like pajama pants and were cut as consistently wrong as possible for her figure; they underscored everything they should have concealed. On her head she had a gigantic brown felt hat à la Garbo, and its long shadow hid her face, an effect which had previously been secured by the hide-and-seek sunglasses. She looked fantastic. I ran across the street and met her at the door of the hotel.

"I rented it," she said. "Nobody knows it's me who rented it. They won't be able to find us through the license plates. Smart, eh? What are you grinning at?"

"You look like a mixture of Garbo and Rivels, with a sprinkle of Napoleon."

Suddenly she stood absolutely still in front of me.

"Garbo and Rivels and a sprinkle of Napoleon . . . You know, that's the best inside information anybody ever gave about me. No one recognized me on my way here. I'm terribly sorry I'm late, but somebody was always calling. I started the car three times, and each time I thought of something I had forgotten, and when I got upstairs there was somebody calling, and there was a message I had forgotten to leave. Good Lord, that's how it is when you want to get away. Are you mad at me?"

"No, I'm resigned to having things happen as they do. Just as long as something happens."

"If that's true, then we're well suited for each other," she said, kissing me as we stood in the open glass door, and the difference between the warm air of the street and that of the cool air-conditioned hotel made the breeze whirl around us.

"Isn't it a good disguise?"

"Hm!" I heard the desk clerk say. "Would you mind demonstrating your 'love' either inside or outside the door?"

We went inside. The desk clerk looked up at us. He stared at her. He stared very hard. Then he straightened up, his hardened face showing as much surprise as it was humanly possible for him to express. With an elegance à la Jacques Tati, he came around the counter to her and took her hand.

"When I was in Europe I learned to say *madame!*"

He kissed her hand in the noblest French manner.

"Welcome, Miss Monroe. This is a great honor to me!"

At first she looked at him surprised, then she laughed delightedly.

"Could you really recognize me?"

"Of course, there can be no doubt that you *are* Miss Monroe. I'm ashamed that I didn't see it before. I am a great admirer of yours. Let me help you and the gentleman out with the luggage."

The desk clerk picked up my poor valise, carried it out to the sidewalk as if it contained gold bars, and put it down among the enormous heaps of clothes and things with which she had filled the back seat. After that he stood straight and saluted.

She patted him on the cheek and he blushed.

"You're sweet. I'll remember you in my evening prayer," she said, ran around the car, and jumped into the passenger seat.

"I'll tell you where to drive. I don't like being the chauffeur."

I started the car and waved to the desk clerk, who leaned over to me and whispered:

"Sir, the next two bottles of Scotch are on me. It's been a pleasure."

We drove across Manhattan, over the Hudson, and into New Jersey, first northward and then west toward the mountains. At first she sat silently coiled up in the corner of the seat, saying nothing. Then she got up and began to rummage through the heaps in the back seat. She fished out a bottle of Dom Perignon, opened the glove compartment and found two plastic cups, undid the wire seal, and worked the cork up, so it flew out of the car and the foam was blown back by the wind. She poured and handed me one cup, drank hers empty in a few big sips, and poured again, placing the bottle between her knees.

She held the cup in one hand, while the other secured the gigantic brim of her crazy hat.

"We're on a holiday now," she said. "For a few days, maybe for a few weeks; I don't know, it all depends, but don't ask me. We'll go up to the mountains where the tall evergreens are. People who have been in Europe say it looks like Norway or Switzerland. There should be a motel somewhere in the woods if we follow this route. Are you happy?"

"Yes, I'm happy. There's a famous Danish poem about 'The Flight to America.' This is my flight to America."

"What's the poem about?"

"About the dream every generation has of fleeing to Paradise."

She poured more champagne.

"You're right, but how strange it is. One thing the world would never believe is that I'm fleeing."

"A flight can end in a new life."

"You're right again. I've decided I want to begin a new life. A completely new life."

"Do you also know what it's going to be like?"

"No, that's the problem. Somebody must help me find out. You, for example."

The road began to snake upward, and it quickly became cooler. We reached large forests of tall, straight conifers, and a dizzying smell of ozone filled our lungs. Again, she clambered over the seat, rummaged through the luggage, and found a beige sweater, which she put on over her white blouse. She threw the hat on the back seat, leaned out over the side of the car, and let the wind blow through her hair until it stood around her face like a wild, white light of curls.

She pulled her head in again, leaned up against me, and said:

"I'm *going* to be happy. Now. You know what I mean?"

"You mean that I should not under any circumstances stop you from it."

"Exactly. Then I won't have any regrets."

Just before dark we reached a motel that lay in a clearing in the woods. The air was cool and clean, and the motel was built in the Swiss style. When I switched off the engine, everything was absolutely quiet.

She remained in the car while I went to the reception desk and got the key, and as I was opening up she found some bottles of Dom Perignon under the valises and entered the room with them in her arms.

"The luggage can wait," she said. "I'm hungry. Bring whatever you can find in the restaurant. Just not spaghetti."

I returned loaded down with chicken, sausage, salad, and cheese, and when I entered the room she was standing naked before a large mirror that was fastened to the inside of the closet door. She stared at herself, deeply interested.

In the mirror she saw what I had on the tray, and she nodded.

"Why do I love looking at myself naked in the mirror?"

"Because you want to make sure that you're still as pretty as everybody thinks you are—which you are."

"Somebody told me it's because I'm n-n . . . something with an *N*, what's that word again?"

"Narcissistic!"

"Right. What does it mean?"

"In love with yourself."

"I *am* in love with myself. Is that wrong?"

"You can't love others without loving yourself," I said, went over to her, and put my arms around her. She took my hands and steered them up to her breasts.

"Do you think they're pretty?" she asked.

24th Day

Very early in the morning—just before sunrise—at the moment I woke up, I could see a green glow edging the dark of night out of the sky. I was awakened by her rattling a glass.

"What are you doing?"

She hung half out of bed and was groping for something on the floor.

"I'm looking for my sleeping pills."

"Now? It'll be morning in an hour."

"I didn't think you'd hear it. You wake up at the slightest sound."

"It's too late to take sleeping pills now."

She rose to an upright position beside me, her movements quick and annoyed.

"I haven't closed my eyes since you fell asleep. I can't stand it anymore. I want to *sleep.*"

"I held you until you fell asleep."

"I pretended to. I was trying an old trick: lying as I'm used to doing when I fall asleep. I breathed exactly the same way. I 'acted' sleeping, but it didn't help, and then you fell asleep on me."

"Well, then we'll begin from the beginning again. Lie down, and I'll touch you and rub you to sleep. Taking strong sleeping pills on top of all the champagne you drank is insane. You run the risk of suffocating, don't you know that?"

"Yes. But I haven't slept for almost a week, and I can't *stand* it; I'm sick from not sleeping . . . And I'm past caring about all the good advice from people who fall away the minute they close their eyes."

"Lie down on your stomach, and let me try."

She looked at me a moment, rebellion in her face, then gave in, and threw herself down on her stomach with an irritated gesture.

"It won't work if you're mad," I said. "Relax, and don't think about anything at all. Drive all thoughts right out of your head. Every time a thought pops up, drive it out, just as—as if a cat had come in and started clawing through everything we've thrown on the floor."

"I would never chase a cat away," she said. "Never."

"Shut up, now, and do as I say."

"During my first marriage I took a cow into my kitchen because it was outside and it was raining."

"You're very funny, but try to do as I say all the same, dammit."

"It's true—that thing with the cow. I would never drive any animal out of the house. I take animals *in*. I love animals."

"Fine, but love whatever thoughts come into your head a bit less than you love animals. Agreed?"

"All right, all right!"

She lay still, and I began to rub her shoulders, neck, and back. I tried to rub peace and calm and security into her scalp with my fingers. But suddenly she raised her head, and said:

"Anyway, they could be good thoughts . . . They don't all have to be worse than cats!"

I sighed very loud, thrust her head down into the pillow and sat on top of her, the better to get at her, holding her pressed between my thighs and knees.

She lay still—for a while. I was beginning to believe that my fingers' search for muscular knots, the pressure of my palms, and the careful kneading of her flesh beneath the skin were working. But suddenly her body began to jerk, and she wriggled her bottom, on which I was sitting.

"No masseur would ever place himself that way on a lady," she said.

"I know, but it's easier for me this way."

"It works the other way."

"The other way of what?"

"Of what your hands are doing. You'll have to make up your mind. Either we do one thing or the other. I've got nothing against the other, if you should be wondering."

I laughed, filled with delight over her, and did the other.

Afterward, she said:

"We have to celebrate that."

"It wasn't the first time."

"No, but it was the first time—that way. If there isn't more champagne, there are a few bottles out in the car."

I got out of bed and confirmed that there really weren't any more full bottles in the room. In any case, I could feel that in my head, too.

"Where's the car key?" I asked. "You were the last one to use it."

"On the toilet table or in the bathroom or under

those clothes I threw on the floor or . . . somewhere else."

I looked everywhere, but the key wasn't there.

"Oh, no," she shouted. "Now I remember. I put it in one of my shoes!"

"In one of your shoes?"

"Yes, of course. I knew I'd never remember where I'd put it, and then I thought I'd have to discover it in my shoe. Ingenious, right?"

"No comment."

"Are you annoyed now? You weren't a bit annoyed a moment ago."

"I am *not* annoyed. On the contrary, I'm happy to know for future reference where the car key will be. That is, you know, very practical when traveling by car."

"Good, Daddy. Even old, conceited men can get wiser. But hurry. I'm as thirsty as that poor cat all those bad people chased out of their house because they didn't want to give it anything to drink."

I was on my way out.

"Did you hear what I said?" she called after me.

"Yes, goddammit."

I opened the door and looked out. There wasn't a soul around, so I ran out to the car naked and opened the trunk. It was jammed with a huge pile of dresses, pants, blouses, sweaters, scarves, worn old shoes, cosmetics, pill bottles, bags, hats, books, coats, stockings, robes, bags with hairpins about to fall out of them, hair dryers, curlers, wigs, food cans, fountain pens, papers, skirts, small packages of straight pins, safety pins, needles, a plastic bag with balls of yarn and one with bras —when the hell had she thought of using those?—and —underneath it all—a small stock of Dom Perignon.

I took one bottle, slammed the trunk shut, and took

a deep breath. It was a glorious morning. I felt I had never breathed such fresh air. The sun was already above the horizon, and the green in the sky had been driven out by a flame that cast a glowing reflection over the mauve-colored bark of the mighty spruces. Inside the forest thousands of birds were calling each other like a symphony orchestra sounding out instruments just before the conductor taps his baton.

When I got back, she was sitting upright in bed, naked and a bit swaybacked.

"I know why you took so long," she said.

"Yes, but I'd like to interpret it for you: to be with you is to be constantly paralyzed with surprise at the things experienced."

"I had packed it all in suitcases at first, but there wasn't enough room for them—that's why I was late—so I finally dumped the whole mess out, and then suddenly there was room for it all. And now everything will be much easier to find, and I don't have to be always opening and closing suitcases. Didn't you once say something to the effect that I wasn't really so crazy at all?"

"Yes, something like that."

She held out her glass, the cork shot up, and I poured. Then I went over to the window and opened it so she could hear the birds.

"Can you hear them?"

"Mnnh! But they'll stop singing when the day breaks and the traffic begins again. That makes me think of . . ."

I heard her try to refill her glass, but the attempt ended mostly on the blanket.

". . . myself . . . Did I ever tell you that I like to write poems?"

"Yes."

"I like to best when I'm about to get drunk. Sad, because then I can't. Couldn't you write the poem I would like to write? This thing about the birds that suddenly stop . . ."

I went over to her, and she finished the glass in a hurry before I took it, then tossed herself back on the bed, rolled over on her stomach, closed her eyes, and mumbled something unintelligible. I sat down by her, put my hand on the back of her head, and tried to will some of my own tiredness over into her. A faint smile came upon her lips, and she drew her breath as she did when she was asleep.

When I stood up, very cautiously, she didn't awaken. I closed the window and drew the curtains carefully across it, dressed as quietly as I could, and went out of the room, but turned back, found myself a piece of paper, and wrote her:

How the hell are we going to find a common rhythm in all of this? But when you wake up and I see you again, all I can think of is that your eyes are the color of robins' eggs and that you understand the singing of birds. There's juice in the refrigerator. Love, H.

I went down along the highway and wanted to get into the woods, but it was fenced off with a *No Trespassing* sign, and there were no paths visible through the trees. I chose a moment when no cars were coming by and climbed over the fence, fell down into a thick under-growth and began to edge myself through. It was a forest that didn't care for humans. Thorny branches grabbed at my pants and wet leaves drenched them. Between the tall trunks and the dense underbrush, I had become disoriented before I knew it. This was the endless land. I stood still, and after some while, when my breathing had become calmer, I could hear the cars far away, so I sensed which way to head and found the fence again. I went back to the motel, but it was quite a distance; I must have taken a long detour in the woods. My mind and body were tired, there was an unslept sleep in my eyes, and I was hungry. And yet I was filled with boundless happiness thinking about her. It was as if she were the first woman I had met. But that was demonstrably not so. I felt my happiness with her to be larger than myself, like the woods and the vast country around me. It was also sadness that I allowed myself to feel, for our story was a doomed one. It could last only a short while, even though she may have felt from time to time that we were well suited for one another. I didn't know if she had thought that way, and I knew she wouldn't answer if I asked; I didn't want to ask, anyway. I just wanted to be there, near her, as long as I was allowed. She was everything—not only a part of me, a part of what is called beauty and sweetness and femininity; she was all of it, and she was an incomprehensible wholeness in a life that was shattered. She was different from all others, so much different that she was all of them at once. She was, forgive me, the mythical Earth Mother, and anything mankind knew could flow from her. In her eyes I could see the earth being created, I could see myself being born. I could throw myself into them as if into the Stygian waters and come out of them again, up to life, washed of a past, with a mind as naked as a baby crying for the first time. I touched her, and the eroticism of my caresses became love for everything in this world. She didn't belong to me alone; she belonged to everybody. When we were closest to one another, when I was inside her, I was transformed from being one person to being all persons, even though what was happening was an act of love like any other; there was nothing mystic, unusual, unintelligible, inexplicable. We were like any other loving couple, but she made our love into a symbol. That's how I felt that strange morning.

I could indulge in writing about the peculiar color of her eyes, compare it with the purest light blue I have ever seen at sunrise in the Sahara Desert. I could write about her skin and say it flowed over my fingers like milk. I could tell about the tightness of her sheath, about the light weight of her breasts, and say there was laughter in her bottom, rhythm in her mouth when I kissed her. But all that was just coincidental and wouldn't describe her; she couldn't be confined within any description. It's only because she's so famous and therefore, to any man that comes near her, an enlargement of himself to a dream everyone dreams, to a *fata morgana:* one can see it, one can plainly see it, although one knows it isn't there. I could have thought that way, and then everything would have been explained. But it wasn't. That was *not* the explanation. All I had to say was that she was a joy that grew in me like a tree that grows up into the sky, and that she was, because deep inside herself she was as transcendentally as nature; she *was* nature—the one that's been lost, the one we abuse, the one we subjugate because we won't admit our limitations. But if I said that, all those who knew her only slightly would reply that I was out of my head, driveling. I felt she was the only human being I had met, and ever would meet, who possessed the pride that consists of being true to her own limitations and who was keen-eyed enough to see her own fate and bow to it. But no one would believe me if I said that. I would be quickly categorized with the usual love-struck fools who make gods of their incidental lusts, and that would be the end of the story, everything explained.

When I got back to the motel I went into the restaurant which, to my surprise, was nearly filled with guests. I found a table, got myself a double portion of eggs and bacon, and was just about to wolf it down, when a man came up with a tray of scrambled eggs and Coca-Cola, asking if he could sit at my table. I would have liked to say no, but it's not done.

"Bill," he introduced himself. "I saw you arrive last evening," he said. "I must say you have a beautiful wife. In fact, she looks like Marilyn Monroe."

"I'm sorry to tell you she isn't, but I'm quite satisfied with her as she is."

"Well, I didn't really think it was her either, but . . ."

Then I saw her. She came through the swinging door into the restaurant, wearing blue jeans that looked as if they had been painted on her and a white blouse on which only the lowest button was buttoned, her hair like burning platinum around the lovely head. She looked for me, found me, sent me a smiling kiss, and came toward me. The restaurant fell silent. Knives and forks were suspended in midair, mouths stopped chewing.

Damn her. How could she? I saw everything crumble around us—around me. If only one of them felt sure it was she, he would sell the news, and in a couple of hours we would have a host of newspapermen after us. And that would be the end of—of everything.

I got up very quickly and went to meet her, stopping her in the middle of the restaurant and whispering:

"Have you gone crazy?"

"You thought I was ugly yesterday in those stupid pajama pants and the Garbo hat. So. Just give me some money, and I'll go to the counter myself and get what I want. I'll take care of myself."

"Wouldn't you rather—"

"Come on, give me the money."

I pulled a few dollar bills out of my pocket, gave them to her, and went back to the table annoyed, upset, sick, sick, sick of it. I sat down tight-lipped and cut up my bacon as if it were her I was slashing.

Slowly, the restaurant began eating again. There were whispers and putting-together of heads, and the men turned around in their chairs and stared at her. When she returned with her tray of hot dogs, cheese sandwiches, and juice, the food stuck in the throats of a score of men. This *had* to end in a catastrophe.

Bill got up, extended his hand, said hello, and introduced himself.

"Hi," she said.

"I'm a truck driver," he said to her. "I parked outside and slept in the truck. I transport grand pianos from New York to Chicago, and I usually stay here overnight. It's the prettiest spot on the way, and the food is good. I was just saying to your husband that you looked a hell of a lot like Marilyn Monroe."

"That's not so strange, because I'm supposed to."

"What?"

"I'm her stand-in; you know what a stand-in is?"

"Yeah, it's the ones who do the rough jobs which the big stars don't want to do themselves, right?"

"Right. It must be cold for you to sleep out in the truck?"

"Nah, I bundle up pretty good, and I save the price of the room."

"I once knew a truck driver. He drove from New York to Los Angeles and back once every week. It must be a hard job."

"Well, it isn't worse than any other job—and something's always happening. Like now, for instance. Marilyn Monroe's stand-in. But you must be kidding! You mean jumping out from the third floor and racing cars through New York traffic during rush hour, that sort of thing?"

"Yes, among other things. I haven't yet tried jumping out from the third floor, but I'm sure it'll come to that. But believe me, there's also a lot of boring stuff in that job. Before Miss Monroe is filmed, I have to play the whole scene through, from beginning to end, to make sure everything is all right for the real shooting. And she always takes so long getting herself ready that I have to do it over and over again, even if it's only to kill time for the rest of the crew."

"Tell me, is she really as terrific as she looks on the screen?"

"Ask my husband; he knows her."

Finally, he turned to me, still more amazed if possible.

"*You* know her? How did you manage that?"

"I'm a script writer," I mumbled sourly.

"Now, tell the gentleman whether she's really as terrific as she is on the screen," she said, kicking me under the table.

"Yes, she is, but she's damned impossible to have anything to do with."

"Impossible? What do you mean? She's the prettiest little thing I ever saw." A slightly threatening tone came into his voice.

"She never does anything but what she wants. She won't listen to good advice—"

"Maybe she knows better herself."

"No."

"How do you know?"

"I just know."

"That's not true, is it?" he asked her.

"Yes and no. She's got nothing against listening to suggestions. But she knows more about films than almost anybody else so she's usually right when she won't do what they say."

"Now, there you see. I thought so. Do you get angry at her?"

"Sometimes, yes."

"Oh, you shouldn't be. No one, out of the millions that see her movies, is mad at her . . . You ought to be ashamed of yourself, you who have the chance to be together with her. Damned if I'd ever get mad at her, whatever silly things she happened to do."

He shoveled two gigantic mouthfuls of scrambled eggs into his hatch and looked at her again.

"She's great," he said, chewing carefully. "I've read that she was as poor as a churchmouse when she started and that she wasn't even allowed to go to school. You don't grow that big from nothing unless you're pretty good, right? Your husband shouldn't be so critical of a person who's done what she has."

"I definitely think so, too, Bill. But men are always imagining things, especially about women. They think they're so much smarter. It's going to be some mess the day they discover they aren't at all."

"Don't you ever feel smarter than your wife—that is, if you have one?" I asked.

"Er . . . yeah . . . but that's probably just because I'm sometimes a little mad. Your wife is right, you should think before you start grouching."

Bill got a guilty expression on his face and shoveled in the rest of his eggs.

"If my wife were as smart as yours," he said, wiping his mouth, "then I wouldn't grouch. Especially if she looked as good, too. You're a lucky devil. And somehow I think you don't even know it."

147

"He's finding out," she said.

"Thank God for that. Otherwise, there wouldn't be any justice. But, listen, why is Miss Monroe always divorcing her husbands? If I caught a girl like that I'd be sure she didn't get away."

"They all want to rule over her. You see, that's the pity of it all. Men fall in love with her as she is, and when they've got her, they won't let her be what she used to be. They want to lock her in and make her live like a nun in a convent. And she just won't tolerate that. Not for long, at any rate. And if she didn't rebel against it, it would just end with their leaving her because she no longer was the same girl they'd fallen in love with. And she can't bear being left."

"That's understandable. It's not very nice either. You know, I never really thought any man could be *that* dumb. Well, it's been a great experience, but unfortunately I have to be going. I'm very happy to have met you, Mrs. . . . ?"

"Mortensen," she said.

"Oh, is that Scandinavian or something? I thought so. The two of you talk with an English accent; you're not from the States. I hope you'll be happy here with us. Anyway, you should be happy, the two of you, writing screenplays and being stand-in for Miss Monroe. My God, I've never even imagined anything like it . . . Thanks a lot for today, and good luck!"

Later, when we left the restaurant, she smiled and kissed me, but I couldn't get rid of my anger. We packed, and she put on a black kerchief that completely hid her hair. When we were in the car she pressed the button that closed the top over us and sat so low in the seat that all anybody could see from outside was a woman's head with a big black kerchief.

We drove on in silence.

"Hans?"

I didn't answer.

"I won't do it again, I promise. Then will you be nice again?"

She leaned up against me, put her arms around me, and kissed me on the mouth, and I did all I could to thaw myself out, thinking that Bill was right: It's unbelievable how dumb any man can be.

"You know what we'll do?" she said. "In the next town you'll buy food for a picnic. I've got a basket in the back with knives and forks and glasses and salt and pepper and everything, and then we'll find a place in the state park that's coming up, and we won't go to a restaurant at all but eat all alone. Is that all right?"

We made our purchase, and late in the afternoon we reached the state park and stopped. We found a blanket in the trunk, which evidently contained anything needed to live in this world. We walked along a path until we came to a river and clambered down to it. We camped in between some boulders that would conceal us from anybody going by—a place where the sun shone on us between the trees. She pulled glasses and paper plates and other necessities from the picnic basket, and we buttered our bread and ate and opened the last two bottles of champagne. The boulders were red around us, the water ran quietly over the small cascade, there were no voices to be heard, and it was very beautiful. She crawled up close to me, put her arms around me, and caressed me.

"Love me," she said. "Love me hard. You're a gentle lover, and those are the ones I like best. But this time do it hard, so hard that I hurt."

25th Day

I heard her groan in the bathroom. I knocked and asked
if anything was wrong.

"No. Just a minute, I'll be right out."

When she appeared, she was very pale and went
quickly over to her bed and lay down.

"I'm menstruating," she said. "I'm bleeding terribly.
It hurts. It hurts like hell. I bleed more than most
women, and it hurts me more. You don't know what
pain it is for me every single month. It bleeds so much.
Sometimes I think something's wrong inside me. I can't
hold onto the children I should have. It goes wrong
every time. But they can't find out why. I think I'll die
one day because some incurable illness grows out of my
womb. I think it's a punishment because I'm barren."

She had taken many pills, but I hadn't interfered,
though I was nervous over the way she stuffed herself
with pills—handfuls of them. I sat down at the edge of
the bed, took my own bed blanket, and spread it over
her because more warmth might help. She took my

watching her life go by on the screen . . . If only I could have attached electrodes to her head and recorded that film!

"It's a gift to me, better than any other you could have given me," she said. "You have made me happy again—more than you know."

There were many things I wanted to ask her about, but I didn't because her eyes were like those of a viewer gazing at a drama on the screen: deeply affected and totally oblivious to anything else.

At last she said: "I've studied with Lee Strasberg at the Actors Studio for some years; I've told you that. I've learned a great deal. Lee says I *can* forget myself and become the person I'm playing and that I do so with radiance. But now you want me to play myself, that is, be first myself, then throw away all my feelings and become another who's also myself . . . ? I'm sure it sounds as confused as it is, doesn't it?

"You also know that Arthur is writing a screenplay of 'The Misfits' for me. I don't understand how he can; he must know I don't love him anymore. But he may think it's just an episode, that it's because I'm not quite well, and that when I'm back to 'normal,' everything will be as it was—and maybe it will . . . I'm sorry . . . You may get tired of hearing it, but I haven't promised you anything, have I? I've never lied to you, have I? But that role in *The Misfits*—there's never been a role I've been more afraid of . . . Of all the roles I've had, it's the one that's most like me. With this, you go still farther; you even go so far as letting me act out my own dream—what everybody makes fun of me for . . . It's crazy, but it's also wonderful. Lee says I should be an actress and leave the movies. He believes in me."

She lay still again for a while, stuck her middle finger in her mouth and bit on it a little, took it out, started to say something a couple of times, but thought better of it, until it finally came:

"I'm trying to think through what I'd like to say to you. I'm trying to get it all together, but it keeps eluding me. So I'm just going to say it as it comes. I've told you more than once that I know a lot about films—the film as a form of commercial art. When I say that, I'm thinking of certain situations. I know that when I do such and such, it will come out on the screen a certain way, and I *know* how it will look and whether it will have the right effect. That's why I have all that trouble with my producers and directors and all the others who have anything to say about it. Afterward, they'll admit that I was right—but always afterward. I've had to fight to be permitted to do what I wanted to do, and I've made more enemies than friends because of it, I can assure you. How do I know that kind of thing? I've never gone to theater school or studied film at a university or had a real teacher. I've learned it by myself, and actually I think it's an instinct; actually, it's not really anything I know, it's something I do—lying down. That's not a very good explanation; I can hear that myself. But what's the consequence? That I stick to films. That's where my talent lies. I can get a bad script —and that's exactly what I've just got for the next film I'm supposed to do, and which I *will* do, according to my contract. Anyway, I'll get it fixed up, so it'll be all right. That's one possibility—to continue as I have up to now: in films and films only. But I hate Hollywood. I know that every new film will be a sickness to me, that it'll make for a fight, that they won't understand me, that I'll make enemies—I, who am so afraid and so sad to have enemies. I only want to have friends. I always want everybody to be happy with me and speak well of me, and I really would like most of all to please every-

154

body. But when it comes down to it, I can't, because I don't want to make a bad film. 'So leave the films, come to Broadway, and be a great actress,' Lee says."

She was silent again, thinking. Then she continued: "But I don't dare!"

Another silence.

"Then there's the third possibility—to quit altogether. That's a breach of contract. Give up *The Misfits*. I can't do that to Arthur. Everything is settled, and he's sure it's going to be a great film. Everybody thinks I'm in such a strong position because my films earn millions for the companies. But the truth is different, perhaps partly because I'm so weak myself and always let myself be led by people I believe in and admire. The truth is that I don't decide my life myself. Others make all the decisions: Fate; I only obey. It's true that I rebel now and then; most people think I do nothing else. But it's never the great rebellion—the one for myself, my real self. But, well, there is the third possibility: disappear. Like Garbo. Live a totally different life. Joe is always proposing to me, and there isn't anything that could make him happier than if I married him again, never played in another film, and was just a housewife to him, buttoned up and puritanical, watching television and making spaghetti, sitting quietly and keeping my mouth shut, while they played cards and grinned over sports jokes that I didn't understand a thing about. Or if not Joe—and it couldn't be—then another. Would you take me to Denmark and let me live alone with you and not try to make me do anything that had to do with my former life?"

"Yes."

"Even though you know how unstable I am, that I can never promise anything for the future, because I don't know what I want to do tomorrow?"

"I know how short life can be. I have a couple of scars that you have seen. One learns from things like that."

"When you were in Africa, what did you do?"

"Experienced things."

"You shot animals, but you won't say so because I can't bear hearing about it."

"I shot animals, yes. That was partly my way of living and partly because we were sometimes hungry."

"That's strange. I hate men who shoot animals. But they're always the ones I fall in love with—or marry. The two things haven't always gone together."

"You're a young woman. There's time enough for you to find out which of the three possibilities you should choose. It doesn't have to be here and now. We all try to do our best, but if we concentrate on that *alone,* we'll end up thinking only about the least important, what we don't want."

She turned over on her side and put her hands over her face.

"Dearest, I don't understand that. I would like so much to have one personality. . . ."

27th Day

We were on the road again. She had slept, and as far as I knew on only two Nembutals. The depression that accompanied her menstruation was over, and she looked fresh and happy.

We drove through Virginia and Tennessee. We were heading for Memphis. I had been there before and wanted to go back and get a second impression.

"There's a great Danish writer who has written a wonderful poem about Memphis," I said. "It may have made the town look better to me than it really is."

"That's a good reason. We'll go to Memphis," she said.

Later:

"I like driving," she said. "Most of all along the coast, but even just driving around. I feel best when I'm in motion. Maybe that's why I'm so ill-suited for marriage."

"It *is* possible to be married and in motion at the same time."

"No, not if you're married to a man! They hate moving. I love it. The best thing about buying a house is the time it takes to furnish it. Men only think of getting it over with, so they can settle down with their feet raised, dinner punctually every day, and television and discussions and work. I could be moving all the time, and yet I like to have a home. And then they say I'm nuts and had better come to grips with my ideas and be content with what I have. Men want to make an exclusive relationship out of marriage, but when I rebel against that and go out with others and go to parties and drown in small talk, then I suddenly feel how empty it is, and I want to return to something stable and intelligent so I can learn something. And when I want that they talk over my head because they think I'm good only for going to bed with and I don't understand one iota of what they say. They treat me like a schoolgirl, and ogle me because I'm a shapely schoolgirl, and then they shake their heads and disappear into their brain-talk again. The consequence is that I constantly have to choose between one thing or the other while I don't care for either. But I always end up in the ditch, and that wasn't the intention at all. There was a time in my marriage to Arthur when I had it good. But it still ended up in the ditch. Now I believe it's better for me to live alone. But then I feel lonely and have to have someone near me again. Isn't it hopeless? I think about it all the time; at night, too. That's another reason why I can't sleep—I think. If I can do what you told me before—drive all thoughts out of my head—then I can fall asleep. But it's the thoughts that drive me, and I let them do it so I can get to know them and know myself; so I can finally get to know enough of them and enough of myself so that I'm not surprised anymore by my own thoughts and ideas and questions. If I succeed in that, once and for all, I'll be able to sleep again. And maybe marry a man who can stand me—and whom I can stand. Oh, God, it's so complicated, isn't it?"

"Not necessarily. For some, success comes with age."

"Then I won't be pretty anymore."

"Most great actresses grow more beautiful with age."

"You promise more than life can give."

"Well, let's say, then, it's a possible truth. That's not the worst thing. And for you, everything is still possible."

"I'm not that patient."

"Courage is inherent, and *you* have courage. Patience needs to be learned. And learning comes easily to you. Courage and patience come from the same quality, and you have it."

"I wish it were true. Wish me luck, darling!"

28th Day

In one of the small towns where we spent a night there was only one hotel, and it had an Italian restaurant. The men stood at the bar, and a few lunch guests were eating pizza. An old, hunched woman entered the restaurant with a large basket full of small bouquets that looked like violets. She went from table to table, but everybody shook his head. Finally, she came to our table. She handed one of her bouquets to Marilyn, who took it and smelled it and smiled at the old woman.

"Only twenty-five cents, ma'am," said the old one.

"How much for the whole basket?" asked Marilyn.

"The *whole* basket—"

"Yes, the whole basket."

"Well, let's see, I haven't thought about that, I don't know how many there are . . . Five dollars . . . You think that's too much? I've never sold the whole basket."

Marilyn took a ten-dollar bill out of her bag and gave it to her.

"But I only want this one," she said, smelling the flowers again.

"Yes, but you can't . . . It's not . . . You really mean it?"

"Yes, I'm happy with this bouquet; it smells lovely —and one is worth just as much as the whole basket."

The old lady looked at her, bewildered for a long while. Then she took her hand, kissed it, and said:

"You're a good woman. God bless you."

My thoughts exactly.

29th Day

We were driving through Tennessee. On a green hill on the outskirts of a small town stood a church built in a French style like a miniature Notre Dame. She wanted to go up and look at it. We went inside. We sat down in the pew next to the altar.

"I had a very religious upbringing," she said, after which she sat silently for a long time.

"Are you thinking now that there isn't much left of . . . my morals?" she asked.

"You can only be guilty or innocent to yourself," I said.

"Maybe I understand what you're saying. Or maybe I don't. But I want you to know that I'm *for* marriage! And if you say that sounds funny coming from me, well, all right; I guess it does. But my rule is that as long as I believe in it myself, I ought to keep myself from others. Otherwise, it won't work."

"You mean that you *have* had enough of it?"

"Yes, more than enough."

"How long are you going to hide it?"

"A bit longer. But the truth is that I really have an old-fashioned puritanical view of marriage. I've always wanted to be faithful. It just never worked. I stopped believing in it every time, even though I can't stand the messy Hollywood sex. Is that what you mean?"

"That's just what I mean."

"But it doesn't seem to make sense, does it?"

"It's sensible enough. If we cast shadows, as they say, it's because there's light somewhere in us."

"You never blame me for anything. I love you for that," she said. "You don't want to own me, do you? Like all the others?"

"I don't want to own anybody. I just want you to be happy." I meant it at the time . . .

"It's strange," she said. "When you're wild about having something, you don't get it. When you're not, you do."

30th Day

"The United States comprises 3,615,211 square miles and a population of about 200 million and stretches across the North American continent between the Atlantic and Pacific oceans. The northern border with Canada, some 3,500 miles long, begins in the west at Juan de Fuca Strait and runs along the 49th parallel until the Lake o' the Woods, after which it follows natural boundaries to the upper St. Lawrence River; it then goes along the 45th parallel and the crest of the Appalachian Highlands until it curves southward and reaches the Atlantic Ocean at the Bay of Fundy. The 1,800-mile-long southern border runs from the Pacific coast near the California Peninsula eastward along straight lines until the Rio Grande at El Paso and after that follows the river to its mouth on the Gulf of Mexico."

"Now you *have* gone batty," she said. "Why on earth are you reading that to me?"

"Because it's pretty, don't you think so?"

"Mn—yes, but . . . I'd rather you just passed the ice."

I handed her the ice bucket, which I had brought up from the hotel bar. She put three cubes into her Scotch and wiped her forehead with a towel.

"Yes," she said, laughing. "Actually, it does sound pretty."

"It's a quote from an old, dog-eared encyclopedia which was down in the bar. I looked up the United States while I was waiting for them to get the ice machine to work. Actually, I thought it sounded so pretty that I wanted to read it to you. One way or the other, it *is* a poem. What do you think?"

"I didn't think it was *that* warm here. I can't take too much heat. I can't imagine how I'll sleep in this heat. How could you stand Africa?"

"I can't get enough heat."

"You want it straight on your skin, into you?"

"Yes, I enjoy the sun as you do champagne."

"That sounds like . . . I mean, am I an alcoholic?"

"Shall we say you drink?"

"I may have my reasons."

"One always has."

"You know me well enough to know that I do. Anyway, you shouldn't sit that long in the sun naked. You'll get a burn."

"No, I have a year's training from Africa."

"Do you know you're tanned in a peculiar way? Your tan is yellow."

"That's African too."

"There's something about you and Africa . . . What is it?"

"An old love."

"Unhappy love?"

"That, too."

"You want me to stop asking?"

"Please."

"Good, I don't want to get a sunburn. I want to be a blonde all over!"

We were sitting on an old, rotten balcony in front of our room at the ramshackle hotel we had discovered in Memphis, a hotel that had to date back to the Civil War. We had driven through the Southern states, and with each mile we drove the weather got warmer, life more primitive, history more alive. Racial hatred began to show its face. The motels became shabbier. In the hotel in Memphis, by that grayish-green, slovenly, muddy, dirty Limpopo River, which here was so beautifully called Mississippi, the balconies hung down toward the stream, dry-rotten and moss-grown like the banks of the river. The heat was heavy and humid, and she sat naked in the shadow under a torn, frayed awning in an old, knock-kneed deck chair, a towel in one hand, the ice bucket at her side, and the bottle of Scotch in her other hand like an oversize piece of jewelry that had grown fast to her fingers.

The smell of the South *is* an African smell: dark, silent, persistent, heavy, humid, steamy—a smell of wet, sweet grass, like that rising from an ironing board when the iron sizzles over newly sprinkled cloth. The river was somewhat putrid, the long pontoon boats with their loads of cotton bales lay waiting to be sent on, things had apparently come to a halt. But behind the standstill it looked as if the decay possessed its own growing life. The language, too, had changed—the vowels edged out the consonants more and more. The nights became hotter and heavier, the days more colorful. People going by no longer walked with an Eastern Seaboard briskness; they sauntered or lay down to sleep. There was always a siesta, but behind the sleeping or waking faces, be they closed or bursting out in black laughter, the passions were rising, and I felt the same was happening to us—that we were coming close to an explosion. But everything pointed to the contrary. She lay limp and tired and sweaty in the musty deck chair. The sun and the heat and the life-style of the South had already penetrated our bodies, and we were far away— much farther than the distance we had traveled—from the life we had just come from. Far off in a bar a band was playing the "St. Louis Blues."

I had decided to keep an eye on her pill popping; she evidently didn't realize how dangerous it was. Day in and day out she would be taking pills for headaches or stomachaches. At night she would stuff herself with Nembutals to fall asleep. Late in the afternoon, when she finally woke up, she took pills to be fresh and alert. She took pills for constipation, for twitching in her legs, for pain in her chest, and she took diet pills, dehydrants, and a dozen other medications that were supposed to clear her skin, freshen her blood, strengthen her bones, etc., etc. All this was washed down with Scotch or Dom Perignon, provided we could get it. She could gulp down a bottle of Scotch faster than the biggest, burliest steersman of a Mississippi riverboat. Not long after we began our odyssey through America it became clear to me that it was certain death to let her sit behind a wheel, even though it gave her hands some sort of occupation.

I had tried to explain to her how dangerous barbiturates and alcohol were.

But she wouldn't listen.

I had told her she would ruin her beauty prematurely.

But she wouldn't listen.

I had kept my mouth shut and let her do as she pleased, thinking that it wouldn't last. But the pill case was always the first thing to be taken out of the car, and

I knew only too well that sequence of movements: the hand with the pills, the mouth filled with water, and the throw back of the head; and I realized that she was deep into something far more dangerous than she imagined. She also felt justified. Why in heaven's name should she suffer pain when it wasn't necessary? Why should she put up with lying sleepless at night? Why should she look all puffed up in the face if it could be gotten rid of artificially? What had these pills been made for anyway? Would her doctor give her the prescriptions if they were dangerous?

I explained over again as quietly and unpreachingly as I could.

But she wouldn't listen.

And the Scotch?

I couldn't afford to talk.

I got up and went to the bathroom to wash off my perspiration. When I returned and was drying myself, she threw the empty bottle of Scotch into the river.

"Can't you go down to the bar for another?" she said, falling back heavily on the deck chair, so one more rent appeared in the musty sailcloth.

"No."

"If you won't, then I'll do it."

"You won't."

"Yes, I will, and I'll go down just as I am, like this—" She rose a bit unsteadily, wrapped the bath towel around her, and paraded past me like a Cleopatra.

"My head is very clear right now. I feel marvelous. You don't know how many good ideas I've had. In my head I can see everything we should do, so why the hell shouldn't we drink another bottle while I tell you everything I've f-figured out . . . ?"

"Because you can't take it. You shouldn't drink that much in this kind of heat. You've been taking pills, too. It'll make you sick."

She put her arms around my neck, and the bath towel sank down around her feet.

"Just one more, Daddy. I can't sleep anyway, and we can talk so nicely if we have one more with ice and soda . . ."

She pressed herself up against me, and I put my arms around her. She was soft and lovely, and she batted her eyes, impossible to resist, and rubbed her sex against mine, her hips and buttocks gyrating. I knew I shouldn't, but I'm only human, and I lifted her up and laid her on the bed, and she crept around me and rolled into me and was what she *was.* Her breasts were soft like gift packages, her tongue scurried around in my mouth like a red sugar ball, and her fingers ran like tickling branches of spruce all over my body—into my ears, my nostrils, and navel—and I caught fire, and my tree burnt out in her. Afterward, we lay side by side, dripping with perspiration and breathing heavily in the sudden darkness of the South, which fell over us like a wet, steamy curtain.

"So go for that bottle," she said.

"No."

She got up enraged, picked her towel up from the floor, wrapped it around herself, opened the door, and went out into the corridor. I knew she would do it and all hell would break loose, so I had to go after her and pull her back. She thrashed and clawed at me, screaming out so I had to put my hand tightly over her mouth and struggle with her until I could pull her back and roll her onto the bed again. But she didn't give up; she suddenly gathered her strength and used it without restraint, like an animal. If I let go of her mouth in order to hold her down, she screamed so loud I was sure it could be heard all over Memphis. The only thing I could do was to sit on her and stuff the pillow into her mouth to stop her screams and hope that she would finally get tired. But she kicked and struggled and snorted and kept on, while the sweat dripped off both of us and the tears of her rage and drunkenness streamed down over her face, usually so pale but now red with anger, until she finally stopped and sank down on the bed without resistance and cried—just cried.

I got coffee for her—lots of coffee—holding the cup for her while she gulped it down. She mumbled something about tranquilizers in the case, and I found them and gave them to her, and soon afterward I got her up off the bed, helped her to the shower, and washed her down with lukewarm water that streamed over her swaying, burning body, suddenly so aged, shrunken, and forlorn. I dried her, put my arm around her, held her very close as we walked out to the balcony, and sat her down in the deck chair, where, suddenly, her teeth started chattering, so I had to wrap her up in every sheet, blanket, and towel I could find and drape my jacket around her shaking shoulders, while she kept on quietly crying—not because she felt terrible or felt ill but because . . . because . . .

"Why isn't there anybody who can make me stop?" she said.

"There are plenty who have tried to help you, aren't there? I'd like to help you too, but you're out there somewhere where you need some kind of born-again religion to make it, you understand?"

She nodded.

"Yes, I think so. But there's nothing in me except what others have put in there. And none of it seems to be what I need. What is it that I need?"

"I've told you before: love. Even though it's hope-lessly banal."

"I've had lots of love. I'm incessantly in love with someone or another. Right now, with you. But it hasn't made me a bit better or smarter and not happier either."

"If you *look* so hard for love, you usually grab rather uncritically on to anything that comes along. It shouldn't come as any great surprise to you that the attempt quite often fails."

"Darling, you mustn't talk so abstrusely. And I'm still freezing."

I lifted her up from the deck chair, put her on the bed again, and put my arms around the bundle of clothes to warm her with the heat from my own body. The balcony door was open; the river was so broad that we could still see it. The gently swaying lamps in front of the hotel and the streetlights on the opposite bank glowed on the viscously flowing water. Once in a while a boat would dream itself by, just gliding off southward with the current. The band in the faraway bar was still playing New Orleans music, but otherwise everything was quiet.

"You mean, if I had found the right one . . . That's just as banal. Is it impossible to discuss these things without being banal? . . . You mean I would then have been, well, happy?"

"Maybe, maybe not. Most of us forget what it was we were looking for after we've found it."

"Maybe I just can't love at all? Maybe I can just long to?"

"That's the case with some people, I know it's not with you. I think there's a tremendous longing in you; it's the innermost core of your being. That much I think I know. It's also the innermost core of your talent.

Everybody who sees you experiences a lonely longing."

"Lonely longing . . ." she whispered, lying quite still and staring out on the black, glistening skin of the river.

She wasn't crying anymore. Suddenly she laughed her mousy laughter and said:

"I've always thought I was too small. It's not only to make my legs look more elegant that I wear high heels. It's to make me taller—even though I get a backache from it, down there in the muscles right above my rump. I've always wanted to learn something, too; I don't know anything. But I listen and ask. I also get answers, and I remember them. But I can't make them all hang together. I can't make them fit into a picture I understand. Won't you lie down beside me now and try to sleep? I'll lie still and not do anything or go anywhere. I'm sorry for what I did. I didn't want to be mean to you."

"And I didn't want to be mean to you. But we both were anyway. I guess that's how it happens with most lovers. Can you forgive me?"

"My darling, do you really think I don't know that the only thing you want is to be good to me?"

31st Day

I fell asleep but slept restlessly: I ought to stay awake and keep an eye on her. In the strange, faintly lit darkness I could see her lying with her eyes open, staring up at the ceiling—sleepless, despairing, lonely—while my own eyes kept closing and I fell asleep again. Early in the morning I woke up with a start. I knew something was wrong. She had disentangled herself from all her wrappings and lay naked on her stomach, her breath a succession of wheezing stabs. I rolled her over and called her name, but she didn't react. On the night table was a container of Nembutals, and it was empty. I pulled her up and shook her, but she didn't open her eyes and didn't react. I dragged her to the bathroom, put a foot on a pail, and folded her over my knee with her head down over the toilet bowl. I tried to get my fingers into her mouth, but it wouldn't quite open, so I held her nose, and she opened her mouth, mumbling something. I stuck three fingers deep into her throat, and she soon began to throw up. I kept at it, while she complained and tried to get out of my clutches, but I didn't let go of her, and the Scotch came up and the pills and finally just gall. I washed her face, put my arm around her waist, and forced her to walk around the room. She complained some more, whimpering and coughing, dangling almost unconscious on my arm, while I walked and walked and walked her around. She was too weak to put up any resistance, and very slowly I felt life coming back into her body. Finally, she opened her eyes, but she had difficulty focusing, and she couldn't answer my questions. I filled her up with water, took her to the bathroom, and got her to throw up again, then back to the bedroom, up and down the floor. Very slowly, she began to breathe in a normal manner, so I could finally lay her down on the bed again. After that I ran down to the desk clerk, put a ten-dollar bill on the counter, and asked him to get me two or three quarts of milk, but quickly, no matter how, just milk and quickly. The desk clerk was evidently used to crazy people, so he just nodded and set off running down the street, returning shortly with a pitcher of milk. She had recovered to the point where she could sit up, and though she vomited still once more, I got the milk into her and let her lie still. She fell asleep at once, but I remained sitting by her side all through the morning, taking her pulse and listening to her heartbeat.

She was over it.

Late in the afternoon she woke up. At the moment she opened her eyes she saw me. She started to cry, very quietly, then took my hands and kissed them and kissed them and wouldn't let go of them.

"I didn't mean to kill myself," she said. "I just had too many pills."

That night she managed to sleep. She had two Nembutals, which I gave to her, and I held her in my arms. She dozed off under my caresses—caresses that forgave, and asked forgiveness.

32nd Day

When she woke up, she was pale and weak. Looking sick, she wandered in a dreamy, listless manner around the room and out to the balcony, where she stood for a long time with two fingers in her mouth, staring out at the river. Then she took a bath—for hours. And she put so much perfume in the water that the scent seeped out under the bathroom door and into the room, blending with the heat, so even the faint smell of decay from the Mississippi disappeared. When she finally came out in her white robe, she sat down before the mirror, brushed her hair for what seemed an eternity, and rubbed that cream onto her face with which she had been anointed the first time I saw her.

I had been out and bought us food for breakfast, but we didn't get to eat it until late in the afternoon. She placed herself, silent and quiet in her movements, in the torn deck chair on the balcony, and we ate and drank juice for a long time without a word.

Then she finally said in a voice that was barely audible:

"I would like most of all to stay here in this closed, strange somnambulist room forever—never again venture out to anybody or anything. But I know that soon I will leave, *have* to leave . . . Is that what makes me so depressed? I want to be alone, and at the same time I'm afraid of loneliness. I want to have children, and at the next moment I think it would be bad for my career, and I can't anyway . . . How many times have I told you that? It must be a trauma. Can you stand hearing me say the same things over again? Yes, you can. That's it. Apparently, you don't even have to make an effort. You just do it. It's different with me; I always make an effort . . . But the motive isn't very pretty . . . It's to be better than everybody else, but I feel that I'm beginning from scratch each time, pulling an enormous load, when I go to the studio for a new film. I feel it's insurmountable; I'm sure I can't pull it off, but I do my damndest—and envy other stars that seem to have luck with them . . . Hans, I'm not anything to cherish . . . I just get older without getting wiser . . . See . . ."

She held out her hands.

"There are already brown spots on my hands, and that's age, and I hate it. I would like to know more, but while I read and try to get smarter, I'm thinking that they're making fun of me, saying I don't understand what I'm reading and can never get any smarter. You said one day that life subsists by its own inner contrasts. If that's true, I'm the most alive person in the world!"

"That's exactly what you are! But I didn't say it was easy."

33rd Day

I hadn't seen her like this before. She moved only between the bed, the bathroom, and the balcony, and all the time like a zombie. It was as if something had snapped inside her but also something had opened up. We felt great love for one another—love that filled our existence with ever more tender affection. I felt that she was trying to make herself even more naked than she was—and she was naked most of the time—but she did it by showing the litheness of her body, by making herself so soft that it seemed as if she didn't have any bones at all.

Suddenly she said:

"I would like to make sex into love, to make sex into something that's not corporeal . . ." And then she started laughing at herself. "And if I could, then *that* would be the mystery they all keep writing about and saying I contain, but which they can't make out. To make sex appear like a dream of love . . . You've discovered it, haven't you? But you'd say it differently, wouldn't you?"

"How's this . . . ? You make sex into Eros. The exact opposite of all the others, the opposite of the times; I think that's why you're such a lonely fighter."

"I was a fighter once. I don't want to fight anymore, but now it's impossible to stop. I wish my heart could melt like ice in my mouth."

34th Day

"This mirror is much too small," she said. "You've got to get me a bigger one—full length."

The hotel manager proved to be very understanding.

"We don't see very much of your wife, but I'm told she's very beautiful. That sort of lady should have a large mirror. We'll find one."

There weren't too many guests at the hotel; its better days were long gone. But the mirror that two hotel porters lugged into our room was certainly from halcyon times. It was enormous, mounted on lion's-claw legs, and movable in all directions.

She planted herself, satisfied, in front of it.

"What do you think is the prettiest about me?"

"First I thought it was your eyes. But when someone knows all the tricks the way you do, with black and blue and drops and lines, then, fantastic as they are—and I've never seen any woman with *that* kind of light-blue eyes—well, it could be more a good makeup job than nature. Then I thought: It's your hair! But the truth is, you're a brunette. It's more than a week since you've been to your hairdresser, so one can begin to suspect that the platinum is produced . . ."

"I thought you loved me."

"Precisely. To those we love, we risk telling the truth, and then we get to know if we in turn are loved! After that I thought—that was a bit later—that it was your breasts, and it's true, they're large and elegant and set high and soft and lovely. But really, so many women's breasts are; no one can become so famous for beauty as you are because of them."

"Thanks a lot!"

"Oh, stop pretending! You know very well it's going to be good in the end. Anyway, then I really thought it was your behind; you've got a magnificent ass. It doesn't hang, it's firm; there aren't too many who possess that kind. There's calypso in it; you can be proud of it, but that's still not what makes you an exceptional beauty. It's your back. Your back is perfect, contrary to what is the case with most women, whose back is the part of their body they're most in need of hiding. Your back is classic, noble, genuine; it's simply *impossible* for you to play any tricks with it, and it isn't necessary either. Any director, any dressmaker, or anybody who gives you a dress or a bathing suit or anything that hides your back commits sacrilege against beauty. It's in your back that Venus lives."

She turned around and mirrored her back, turning her head as far as it would go without breaking her neck, and inspected her posterior side.

"Nobody has said that to me before. Not *that* way, at any rate."

"Not all men are equally observant," I said smugly.

"There could have been women, too."

"I don't think you've had too many girlfriends."

"No, none. All my 'girlfriends' have been male. But there have been a couple of hundred photographers who have taken pictures of me. They should have seen it."

"They'll discover it, there's still time."

"I'll see to it that they discover it . . . Then, that must be the reason you like to massage my back and I have to lie on my stomach all the time? Or—"

"Shall we say *almost* all the time?"

"Well then, dammit, *almost* all the time?"

"Yes."

"I really can't stand men!"

"You've managed to hide that idiosyncrasy pretty well."

"Idiosync—what's that?"

"Let's say 'dislike.' "

"That's what I was telling you yesterday; I can never figure out whether I like one thing or another, whether I want this or that, and then the whole thing never comes to anything and I get depressed; because if it comes to anything, it's wrong. I fall in love easily, and I like it, and I also like to go to bed with them, but then I discover that they're not interested in me at all but in themselves; they're after something, or they think it's enough to be good-looking. The hell with their good looks; I don't give a hoot how they look. I want men who are courageous, honest, and talented, and wear glasses and have crooked teeth if it so happens. I'd rather do without men than be together with men I'm lonely with."

"Thanks for that about the glasses and the crooked teeth; that fits me beautifully."

"And I thank you for that about my back . . . Why did you tease me like that before; I don't like being teased."

"Because you're in a good mood today. You feel good today. You're getting better. You can get over depressions, too, even very quickly; in fact, so quickly that you may be a bit ashamed how miserable you were just a short time before."

"You say some clever things every once in a while, I'm sure, but I promise you I don't want to be 'educated.' There *are* a couple of writers who have tried. I've had more than enough of it."

"It doesn't seem to be necessary either."

"Bull. Now you're saying something *stupid;* it *is* necessary, and you know it. You're just flattering me."

"Naturally. Why should I do otherwise? Was it *very* uncomfortable for you that I said you had the most beautiful back in the world?"

"You didn't say that."

"I said it was the seat of Venus. It's the same thing."

"Darling Hans Daddy, would you like to touch it?"

"Yes."

"Be my guest."

35th Day

This was the day it happened. I had always known it had to. She couldn't keep running away, and the day had to come when she wouldn't want to run away anymore. She called Fred. He was so angry that I could hear the sound of his voice coming from the telephone across the room and out on the balcony, where I was sitting and waiting to hear when it would all be over.

"I must call Fred," was all she had said, in a voice that didn't veer from the close-to-a-whisper style—a trifle sad, a trifle aggressive, a caress and a fact at once. I had just nodded. I knew all the thoughts that had gone through her head before she had managed to say it.

She fought hard. First she got a hullabaloo over how she had vanished, where was she, what was she doing, what had she thought of doing, and then the whole jeremiad that he no longer could put Fox off, that he couldn't invent any more lies and excuses . . . Well, it wasn't Fox alone either, she knew that very well . . .

And yet I could also hear in his voice that fat, pleasant, congenial Fred didn't mean anything by his anger and really was entirely on her side, but he thought he was using good psychology to persuade her to do what he was sure was the best for her. As to the rest of it, he knew very well what she was doing, and he knew she knew he knew it, and that he would cover for her and defend her against anybody. There wasn't a lie that he, in his jovial, confidential manner, hadn't used and with considerable success. People actually believed him. (Didn't he himself, too?) So she forgave him all his patriarchal assaults.

I turned around only once to look at her. She was sitting with the receiver pressed to her left ear, wearing a white bikini bottom, a blue blouse with colored figures hanging loose over her naked torso. Her hair, which hadn't been done for more than a week, resembled the soft curls of a lamb's coat. Her right hand was pulling at the curls in a hopeless, unconscious attempt to straighten them out, which only tousled the hairdo still more. She gazed down at the floor with a distant look in her eyes, but she didn't see it. In her eyes and around her mouth there was the beginning of a smile.

"All right, Fred, all right, so let's say . . . Tomorrow?! I can't. Good heavens, I've got to have a day to make myself presentable, that's impossible . . . You're leaving today? Okay, then you can prepare everything . . . Let's say four days . . . ? Yes, I *did* say four, and that's how it'll be, and you have to fix it for me; I *can't* any sooner . . . No . . . yes . . . maybe . . . I don't know, don't pester me now . . . Fine, we'll say that. 'Bye, Fred!"

She came out to the balcony, sat down by my side, and looked out on the river.

"Did you hear . . . ? Four days."

"I heard. You don't have to say any more. It's okay. I knew."

"You knew . . . that I had to call today?"

"Yes."

"But I didn't say anything."

"I have feelings."

"I do, too. It's quite unbelievable how . . . You know I can sense in advance what will happen? I usually can. I also know what other people think and feel and intend to do, even though their faces don't show anything. I know what they *would* say if they were honest and dared to; I know when they're lying, and when they try to put something over on me."

"Unfortunately, they have succeeded quite often in spite of it."

"Yes, but that's not because I don't know it; it's because I don't want to hurt them and contradict them or anything like that. Occasionally, I also know what people are thinking and doing, even though they're far away—from the East Coast to the West . . . It's a bit unnerving . . . Just imagine if somebody knew the same about me!"

"You mean you usually have something to hide?"

"Do I, though! You know that. Think of the two of us—and what would happen if anyone knew about it!! Oh my!"

"Do you see that old riverboat down at the quay?"

I pointed, and she leaned over the railing, looking down the river toward Memphis harbor.

"It's an old showboat. Imagine that—still some of them left!"

"It's no showboat. It's a river liner. It goes from Ohio to New Orleans and back, and it takes fourteen days. It's done that for a hundred years, exactly the same, up and down the Mississippi. It's the slowest, most exciting means of transportation in America—and there's a big wooden wheel at the stern. The lady's name is *Delta*

Queen. She is very noble and spacious, and we'll go aboard tonight, and tomorrow we'll sail to Natchez. From there you can fly to Hollywood—or wherever you're heading."

"I don't believe you. Now you're trying to put something over on me. That kind of thing doesn't exist in America anymore."

"Wait and see. America is more than what you think."

"Why hasn't anybody ever told me this? It's wonderful!"

"Few people are observant, especially when it comes to what is right under their noses."

"Did you arrange for all this already?"

"This morning while you were asleep, yes. We pack and board this evening. It doesn't rock, so you won't be seasick."

She sat down on my lap, put her arms around my neck, and kissed me.

"When are you going to do something wrong? Sooner or later you'll *have* to. Did you know that I'm in love with you?"

"You're not very good at hiding it."

She laughed, happily—happy because something she'd been afraid of had suddenly disappeared.

"Have you made any other decisions about what I should do and when?"

"Yes. If you'd look the other way, over at the tents on the far side of the river."

"Aye-aye, sir."

"It's a circus. There's a lady who has skin like an alligator, a merry-go-round, a shooting gallery or two, ten bars, and finally Elvis Presley himself!"

We went across the river by boat. She was wearing black silk pants, flat shoes, the blue blouse, a blue kerchief, and large sunglasses, and she was not recognized —which didn't mean that the men weren't looking; her loveliness came through any disguise. She wouldn't be very pleased if it didn't, I thought. And one day she would throw away her disguise in an incontrollable urge to be Marilyn Monroe.

We sat at the rear end of the long, low boat. The rail was just about eight inches above the water, and she let one hand run through the current, while her face was turned toward me. Her sunglasses were so dark that I couldn't see whether she was looking at me or out on the river.

"What are you thinking?" she asked.

I told her.

She turned her face away and looked at the other passengers, into some of the eyes that were staring, and back at me.

"I'm trying to find an answer for you," she said. "But I can't express it the way I want to. I'm always using words that—well, say something different from what I want to say. But if I find the words, I'll tell you."

"There are alligators in the water," I said.

She shrieked abruptly, frightened, and her hand shot up. She became pale and breathless and stiff with fear —until she saw me grinning.

"Oh! you're teasing me again. I've told you you mustn't. You scared me."

"I'm sorry, take it easy. They told me the same thing the first time I was here; it's a kind of welcoming joke. Please, darling."

"I know; you're forgiven. I'm a chicken. I'm afraid of everything, most of all if it's got something to do with death."

For safety's sake she looked intensely over the water and beyond to the riverbanks.

"There are three things I'm deathly afraid of," she said. "Drowning, choking, and alligators. They stink of death. You're sure that—?"

"Yes, quite sure."

The boat moored on the other side. We were the last to disembark, and we kept to the rear, walking slower than the others, so we were soon alone. On the way up the incline she saw a bench under a big mangrove tree. She took my hand and pulled me over to it, and we sat down and looked at Memphis and the cotton fields and at the warehouse areas with their large cotton bales and the low barges on the ocher-yellow river.

"I'd like to answer your question, but it's difficult," she said. "Of course, I like my fame; it would be ridiculous to say anything else. Who doesn't want it? But believe me, I *have* had it, I know it's nature; it comes and goes, and one day it'll leave me, too. I know how fickle it is, and maybe it'll be a relief when it happens, if only because I'm afraid of crowds, the hordes of people that press in on me. I've been terribly scared a few times that they would skin me alive, tear me to pieces—once they almost drowned me . . . It's strange how you can feel threatened to death by the best things you do."

She turned away from me and stared out over the river again, put two fingers in her mouth, and nibbled at them.

"I'm hopeless when it comes to answering questions. I can't tell you how scared I am of being interviewed. Afterward, when I see what I've answered, it isn't at all what I meant to say; it's not the truth. Have I said that before? Dammit, put up a camera, and take a few pictures; they'll tell you everything."

"Will they?"

She looked at me in surprise.

"Are they wrong, too?"

"They show what you wanted to show, at *that* moment."

"And that's not the truth either?"

"It's your way of life; stick to it. We have two characters: our own and the one attributed to us. The second one got to be so dominant that it crushes the first."

"You mean I don't exist anymore, that Norma Jean is dead, and that I'm just a product of others and all that they wanted of me?"

"No, I don't mean that, but you're not through fighting to learn to know yourself. You still have some way to go. Come on, let's go up there and look at the lady with the alligator skin and Elvis Presley."

We went through the turnstile and into the crowd of onlookers. She clung to my arm, looked down at the ground, and walked sideways to protect herself from the crowds; something seemed crushed inside her. I took her into a bar tent and asked for two straight bourbons. They were slammed down on the wet zinc counter, and we drank them down in one gulp. The liquor helped. She smiled rather weakly and shook her head.

"It's crazy," she said. "But I don't want to look at the lady with the alligator skin."

"Then we'll take Elvis instead."

We were in the middle of a large crowd. There were toothless old farmers with corncob pipes, young bow-legged horsemen in decorated boots, respectable blue-clad gentlemen with fat women on their arms, black girls wrapped in yards of gaudy cotton cloth, whistling youths, private-school girls in uniforms, winos looking for a bench, players on their way to the next gambling joint, and an elementary-school class holding hands and led by a straight-backed schoolmistress. And there was the baking sun, the dust in the nose, eyes, and mouth, the smell of the steamy river and of dry cotton, hoarse voices, loud voices, shrieks of children from the merry-go-round, mechanical tinkling from the gambling wheels—and the tent with Elvis Presley. The concert had begun. We purchased standing room tickets at the rear of the tent, climbed up the steep flight of steps, and stood in the swaying tent with our back up against a rocking wooden post. We looked down on the stage where the white, pink, and light-blue spotlights flickered over Elvis, who was wearing tight pants like a ballet dancer with a bulging penis constrained inside, he had a duck-tail hairdo with sideburns, and the sweat was pouring down his face as he talked and sang his rock-rock-rock into the microphone, the guitar hanging on his stomach as if it were his only garment, and he kept writhing and thrusting forth his pelvis as though he was having sexual intercourse with the entire audience. The young people in the front rows screamed and rocked with the rhythm. Others—unappreciative, confused, shocked—followed the provocative scene with bulging eyes, while the mass seducer, with his rock rhythm, his penis, his sweat, his orgiastic voice, beat down all resistance and drove the human sheep before him, either out of themselves to become like him, or inward behind wet, frightened faces that dared do nothing, only looked. "Don't Be Cruel" boomed out over the audience, and the tent posts and America rocked in the love-hate rhythm of the new music: kiss-me, beat-me, take-me, rule-me, rule-me, rule-me, yours-mine, yours-mine . . . I had my arm around her, around her hips, which she pressed hard up against me, and I sensed how the jungle drums got to her, even though her face was strangely expressionless, and she seemed exhausted as though she had just run a long way. She listened breathless, her mouth open, but the rhythm had gripped her; she was moving up against me and away from me as if we were dancing, while something in her didn't want to, because she held her arm over my back, squeezing it around me as if she were afraid of being torn away and falling and drowning in a flood tide. When there was a break she wanted to leave. I had to keep my arm around her as if she were intoxicated, and we pushed our way through the swarm of people to one of the bar tents, and another straight bourbon helped her over the paralysis, while I stood close to her and sheltered her from the others, and she huddled over, covering herself, and didn't look at anybody.

Shortly afterward she said: "I'm wild about dancing, but I've only been married to men who couldn't dance and didn't want to—at least, not the last two. Dancing with them was like going across the room, picking up a statue, trudging it over to the other side, and putting it down. I always make the wrong choices!"

"If they'd been able to dance, there would surely have been something else wrong with them."

"You mean then they would have been stupid or mean or bad to me?"

"Maybe. They weren't, were they?"

"No. Would you like to go back to the hotel? I can't take any more of this."

The sun was low in the sky, and our shadows quivered out over the waters of the river, which looked as if it were filled with oil—heavy, smooth, dark. She didn't dip her hand into it. There was a paleness in her face that showed through her makeup.

When we got back to the hotel, she tore off her clothes and took a bath. Meanwhile, I went out, bought a few suitcases, emptied the whole heap from the trunk into them, returned the car to the rental agency, went back to the hotel, and began to pack our things—her things. I left one suitcase empty for everything that had to be collected from the bathroom, and asked her, shouting, what she wanted to wear. White slacks, a white blouse, white shoes, a white kerchief. I found it all, laid it out, took a large bath towel from a closet, and went in to her. The water in the tub was covered with lather, and it ran down her arms and her one leg that was sticking up from the water.

"Finish up now, we have to board in an hour."

"That Elvis Presley," she said. "He just does exactly what he wants. I never do that. Remember I told you?"

"You've done nothing else for a week."

"A week! Certainly, sir. Exactly. I have stolen one week for myself from myself. That's a fine outcome— for a star."

"Finish up now, and quit philosophizing."

She sulked a little and then stood up and got out of the tub. I dried her, and she wrapped the towel around herself and went into the room. She immediately caught sight of the new suitcases and pointed at them.

"They're not ours!"

"I just bought them for everything that was in the trunk."

"Oh God, then I won't be able to find anything any-more."

"I assure you, everything is in the same magnificent chaos as it was before."

"You're beginning to push me around. I can't stand being pushed around."

"I don't push you around. I love you."

She stood still and looked at me. Then she smiled— at me, at herself, at everything—ran over to me, put her arms around my neck, and kissed me. Her scent re-minded me of the sea.

We drove to the *Delta Queen* in two taxis, one for ourselves and one for the luggage, walked up the rocking gangway, past the lower deck with its cotton bales and passengers with chickens in cages and crawling children, black and white, and behind us followed a row of black deckhands with our suitcases on their shoulders as if it were a safari. We climbed up to the top deck to our cabin, which had a screen door to keep out insects. The cabin was paneled with shiny mahogany, with a washstand and an old, blue water pitcher and kerosene lamps which an affable officer lit for us. She clapped her hands, delighted, rummaged through her suitcases for tip money, which she distributed in large notes, sat on the bed, jumped on it, ran over to the old, dull, oval mirror and looked at herself in it, dipped a finger into the water pitcher, tried the screen door, listening to the little clicks when it opened and shut, stared out through the wire net, and turned to me with tiny mesh marks on her nose, looking like a fifteen-year-old girl.

"For this I'll forgive you anything," she said. "I'll never forget it. Have you sailed on a boat like this before?"

"Yes."

"Where?"

"On the Congo River."

"In Africa?"

"Yes."

"You're in love with Africa. You had a great love there?"

"Yes."

"But you're happy now, anyway?"

"Listen, sweet girl. Things sometimes come if you search for them, and when they come after you have searched for them, then you shouldn't be so foolish as not to be happy about them. You understand that? I'm *very* happy."

"Oh, that's good. You know what, I'm hungry. I'm hungrier than I've been for a long, long time. Can you get them to make veal piccata for us?"

"Sure, ma'am, anything you want!"

"Oh, Daddy, Hans, I'm so happy!"

The *Delta Queen* gave a historical, dignified whistle, the hawsers were thrown, the gangway hauled aboard, and the mighty wooden wheel at the stern began to rotate, beating the water to a foam, which for a while was reluctantly driven up against the current, then lost momentum, and spread like a fan over the stream. Sparks flew like fireflies out of the funnel above us and out over the Mississippi, while we sat on the deck behind our cabin and ate something resembling veal piccata with a Spanish red wine.

"I think I could go with you to Africa," she said. "And sleep under a mosquito net—that's what you do, isn't it?—and just be Hans's girl, the man 'who experienced things'! I've never really seen any of the countries I've been to. I've been in Japan and Korea, and the only thing I remember is uniforms and glass doors to hotels and aluminum elevators and hotel rooms, all furnished alike. I've been in England, too. You know what I remember? The arrogant face of a sourpuss director. Oh yes, and saying hello to the Queen. They even say I did *that* respectably. But now I'm really seeing things, even though it's dark. It's good I didn't die the other day."

36th Day

Shortly before midnight the riverboat stopped and dropped anchors. In a little while everything was very quiet. The warm, moist air, with a somewhat rotten, steam-filled, sweet smell, forced its way to us through the screen door. She lay in my arms, listening and experiencing everything that happened around us until she fell asleep, having kicked off her blanket. Early in the morning the anchors were weighed, the wooden wheel started, and the entire ship shook with the strain of getting the big, battered, heavy hulk going. Quite contrary to all her habits, she awoke and wanted to get up and out to look. She put on all her white clothes, and we stood together at the railing again in the sharp morning light. The river was brown now, and the stickiness of it made it look like newly turned earth. The banks became greener, with magnolia trees, palms, and giant ferns growing in between the dense, kalelike mangrove woods, and the air seemed to be filled with old perfume.

She wanted to walk around and see the boat, and she said hello to the crew, all of whom had had roles in *Tom Sawyer*. They looked at her a bit puzzled, as if she were familiar to them but they couldn't make out from where. For a long time she stood in the prow, surveying the *Delta Queen*'s majestic voyage as she crawled around a sandbar only inches away and then moved forward again, pushing a floating islet in front of her until the prow cut it to pieces and a part of the islet scraped along the side of the boat. We elbowed our way about the lower deck, around the cotton bales, and past the blacks with their cages of cackling chickens. Some cows were mooing still farther down in the cargo hold, and five or six sheep, which had broken free, were on their own on the center deck, eating the plants the captain's wife had potted along the railing; there was a big row until they were recaptured and tethered.

The riverbanks grew steadily more swampy and lush, and here and there some old, crooked oak trees grew out over the river. Heavily laden pontoon boats passed us by, pulled by tugs against the current so slowly that they were almost at a standstill. We were on our way into a jungle. I held her close to me, her softness following the lines of my body, and she didn't move at all, just stood by the railing and stared, at once tense and relaxed, filled with a mood that took her far away from her usual life, and with an expression on her face that made me think she might later recall this green day as one of the happiest in her life.

She asked me if I would try to get cold champagne at the bar, and I went for it. As I returned I remained standing on the top step of the steep flight of stairs, watching her. She didn't shine only in darkness. She also shone through the hard sun of the South. It wasn't the white shoes, the tight white slacks, the white blouse, the white kerchief, and the pale skin.

"Did you know that you shine?" I said, as I handed her the champagne glass and poured.

At first she looked at me a bit surprised, then understood and laughed.

"Yes. But I don't always. I know what you mean. It's something I can work myself up to before shooting. Or it just comes."

"You're shining now."

"Hmm! Cheerio!"

She held the dewy champagne glass with assurance and elegance, her thumb and index finger around the rim of the glass and the other three down around the stem. She had thin, beautiful fingers and the supple curve of her wrist was worthy of a ballerina.

"Why are we going to Natchez?"

"It's a small town but with a rich past from before the Civil War. But that's not why. I have a good friend there—a French ambassador now connected with the UN. I traveled through Africa with him. In the Sahara. He bought one of the old 'places' from the times of the Confederacy. You'll have fun seeing it."

"Does he know I'm with you?"

"I told him I had a girl with me!"

"And he wasn't surprised?"

"Not in the least."

"You must be quite a womanizer?"

"Not really. But I don't turn my back on what I bump into."

"Just by pure coincidence, huh?"

"Yes, by pure coincidence—remarkable, isn't it?"

"Quite remarkable. Well, I want to be properly introduced to your ambassador. In case you're interested."

She looked at me searchingly to see the effect of her statement, but I only grinned at her. Then she moved close to me again and bent over the railing.

"If you don't want to, we'll skip it," she said.

"We'll go if you want to. Besides, Antoine will think it's terrific."

"Antoine?"

"Antoine de Bressac, yes."

"You shouldn't flatter people, they can't take it," she said. "But they like it. So I don't care a bit!"

When we had emptied the bottle, she took me by the arm and pulled me into our cabin.

I knew she was very fond of it. It was the first time in my experience with her that she noticed where we were. She had gone through the many hotel rooms without seeing them—except for the mirrors. But here she had looked for a long time and touched everything in the old cabin—the English mahogany chairs with their black horsehair upholstery, the mirror over the washstand with its broad, Spanish wrought-iron frame artistically formed in a marguerite pattern around a tree shaped in a cross, the two engravings of the roofs and towers of Seville, the cracked thick marble plate on the washstand . . . She turned to me, gave me a very light-blue glance, and undressed. I felt a happy joy being with her. I had great love for her, greater than I would ever own up to or admit for fear of being too hard hit when, in a little while, she would be gone. I kissed her breasts and knew that my caresses would soon send ripples through her.

Later she said: "This is a closed room of love; it is quite still, and yet it moves. It's wonderful; this room is a part of me. I have great respect for love. It's just so rarely that I've felt it. I would like to live with you."

"That would be difficult, very difficult. You know that."

"Yes, I know it. But I would like to. It's a dream I

have. I would write a poem about it if I could. It comes
to me through this room I always live in like moonlight
through the curtains I have drawn. Doesn't that sound
like a poem?"

37th Day

When the *Delta Queen* moored at the quay in Natchez, we drove inland, again in two taxis, past neglected plantations with white-pillared wooden mansion houses and finally through an avenue lined with oak trees hundreds of years old that had grown together to form a tunnel filled with whispering green light. Long beards of moss hung from the aging branches, and the air was like that of a forgotten temple in the jungle. There were no people, no sounds; we were back in history at a time when riverboats freighted black gold upstream and white gold downstream and sweaty hands carried porcelain from China, tapestries from France, and crystal from Italy up the clay-filled banks and carefully placed slender rosewood bureaus and empire chests in the white houses to please their masters. It was so long ago. The movers were gone, the fields grown over, and no one pruned the trees lining the avenue.

The house stood at the end of the bearded Disney-like forest, with columns spotted by dampness and a large, empty veranda where history had come to a halt when the South lost the Civil War.

Antoine came out and greeted us cordially, bidding us welcome to Petit La Salle.

"Miss Marilyn Monroe, Monsieur Antoine de Bressac," I introduced them.

Antoine looked at her, with merely a hint of an eyebrow raised to his tanned, furrowed forehead, and said as he extended his hand:

"Très amusant!"

Madame de Bressac, who joined us, did the same, but aristocratic courtesy is without class distinction, and the Chinese coffee service was brought out.

Marilyn sat down charmingly, crossed her legs, pulled down her blouse, straightened her back, and smiled courageously.

Antoine began a spirited conversation about the present African situation—all in French. Marilyn didn't understand a word of French, but she tried to act as if she did, and she played it so well that Madame de Bressac asked her in French what role she would most like to play.

I said that Miss Monroe understood French very well, indeed, but preferred to reply in English and translated for her.

"Lady Macbeth!"

(Well, just for the fun of it!)

Marilyn immediately found out that it wasn't fun, so she tried to salvage the situation by adding that of course she didn't wish to play that role right now, but perhaps sometime.

Antoine asked if she were studying drama.

"Yes, whenever I have time for the classes."

"Why are you studying? Would you like to change to the theater, perhaps?"

"Because I've seen my own films," she answered.

(Splendid!)

"What kind of music do you prefer?" asked Madame de Bressac, who hadn't quite understood the humor.

"Judy Garland, Frank Sinatra, Gershwin. And also Beethoven."

"Oh, Beethoven?"

Madame de Bressac asked no more questions. Antoine, on the other hand, was having a great time. But Marilyn was not, and in an excellent Southern drawl—which I had never heard her use, since she, to the contrary, normally spoke with a British accent—she asked me if I would request my friend, Antoine, to see that all our luggage was brought to our room and if he would have the best hairdresser in Natchez call her right away. "And I mean right away." She stood up and whirled around as if she were wearing a great big crinoline and left the room with a not quite successful toss of her lambskin hair.

"Formidable," said Antoine. "She's as elegant as the Tuareg girls, remember them?"

At that moment the Bressac children came in, a young man and a young woman, both around twenty.

"Somebody said Marilyn Monroe was here," they said, out of breath, and looked around in the room.

Madame de Bressac stood up.

"In any case, there was a lady here a moment ago who maintained that was her name," she said, collecting the coffee cups.

Antoine gave me a tour of the house, showed me the old stables and the remains of the original park, which reached down to a branch of the Mississippi River.

"How the hell do you do it?" he asked.

"You find many strange things happen when you're traveling."

"Yes, God knows. Remember when we ran into the sheikh who served us sheep's eyes and ram's testicles?"

"I can still taste them."

By the end of the afternoon I ventured up to our room. She was sitting at a rococo vanity with a large mirror. A hairdresser and his lady assistant were sweating over her hair. A manicurist sat on her haunches in front of her. Strange machines were buzzing, and the room smelled of burnt hair and perfumes, and there wasn't a spot on the floor where I could put my foot down without wading through clothes. All the suitcases had been flipped open and the contents spread about.

"How could you?" she said. "You knew I would make a fool of myself. That inane question. I've heard it before and answered just as foolishly."

"You served them back beautifully, my pet. It fit splendidly."

"For heaven's sake, can't you tell I'm furious?"

"Yes, but that, too, is becoming to you."

"They'll get it," she hissed.

I sneaked away to the bathroom, and working myself through pools of water, wet towels, more clothes, and a few dozen bottles, I washed and shaved, found my dinner suit, dressed, and crept down to the living room. Antoine was waiting for me on the veranda with a Scotch.

"If I were the host," I said, "I would send a bottle of champagne up to her."

"Consider it done," Antoine replied. "Will it be long before we have the pleasure of seeing Miss Monroe again?"

"Very long."

"Good, we have plenty of time. Everything takes quite a while here. That's why life in the South has its own particular quality. Or that's one of the reasons. I once read an interview with Miss Monroe. She said something like, 'Most people destroy beauty because they want it to come down to their own level. They don't know that everybody can be beautiful, each in his own way. But most of them don't allow themselves because they really don't like themselves at all.' She's quite right. It's a clever point and cleverly put. In the South people like themselves. They're possessed of great pride. Well, let's say many are, not to generalize too grossly. That's why there's so much beauty here."

Two hours after dinner was announced ready, she came down. Antoine saved the situation; he didn't need any explanations. Madame was well schooled in the diplomatic métier and didn't bat an eye. The children were waiting in excitement.

Her entrance was worthy of a Broadway gala performance in all its theatricality. She was wearing a shimmering long white dress, which looked as if it had been put on with a spray gun, and to those who knew anything about that sort of thing, it was obvious that there was nothing under it. It was very low-cut. Her hair glimmered with newly applied platinum, and the curls had been straightened and curved down along and inward to her cheeks. The makeup was perfect, her lips moist with some secret lipstick-wax ingredient, her eyebrows drawn high up into the forehead, her nails polished white, and nobody in the world could have the slightest doubt about who was entering, with her swinging hips thrust a bit forward and her back straight though swayed. A gasp went through the room.

She is so beautiful I can't conceive of it, I thought—yes, "conceive," not just understand; her beauty is a picture that glides by but is still there all the time, can never be reached, only seen, the *fata morgana* in its purest sense. Fortunately, Antoine and I had seen *fata*

morganas before. And Antoine jumped to his feet, off-
ered her his arm, and led her to a chair, where he served
her champagne. It was a mad scene. But everything
followed to order. Antoine found, spontaneously it appeared, the subjects she was comfortable with, cleverly
avoided politics and literature, not to mention philoso-
phy—and it wasn't long before the conversation was
revolving around Hollywood, Fox's everlasting errors,
and then—there it came—her childhood. It was given
in just about the same version as I had gotten it. The
children stared at her in gaping admiration, and—fair
enough—she was worth looking at. (And why not let
that be enough by itself?)

*I remember it as if it were one of her films. And that's
what it basically was, too. I believe it was that night that
I saw her for the first time as she really was. Finally, the
human being came out of her many veils, out of the
myth, out of the illusion. But I only fell more in love with
her. It was unfortunate because during those days I was
thinking all the time that in a very short while, perhaps
only in hours, I would never see her again, and I, too,
belonged to those who—like she had in her fighting
youth—wanted to survive. But that could be difficult.
Here she was with her unique talent for being more
beautiful than any other, with her magic for changing
herself into elf and nymph and to make real every fairy
tale, with her genius for making the film reflect exactly
what she wanted it to—and her genius for knowing what
should be reflected . . . And then this primitive, innocent,
frightened, almost identityless little girl, like a mollusk
which by a tragic mistake had strayed into a pack of
hard-shelled predators that were pecking at her . . . She
bled, desperate in her vulnerable pallor, her unprotected
skin . . . Mentally speaking, she was a bleeder; none of*

her wounds would heal, and she was covered with them,
tattooed almost to death with the bites of others, and
anyone would feel an urge to defend her as if she were
their own child, to cover for her, heal her wounds, allevi-
ate her pains, relieve her anxiety so all-embracing, all-
devouring; her eternity, her anxiety . . .

Late that night she wanted to go to a nightclub; there
had to be one, even in Natchez. And Antoine, whom
she had come to trust and obviously liked, was told to
take care of it. He did. On the way there he told us that
he had spoken to the manager, that all reporters and
photographers would be kept out, and that the doors
would be closed as soon as we were there.

When we arrived, she caught sight of a sign spelling
out *Whites Only.* She refused to go in until it had been
removed. It was removed, and in some incredible way
Antoine managed to explain the matter to her so that
she accepted it and entered on his arm.

The bandleader had obviously been notified, so the
minute she entered the band played "Do It Again." It
only took a few seconds before everybody had seen her.
They stood up and applauded, and she waved back and
laughed and appeared to be happy, which she probably
was, too. And when Antoine took her to the dance
floor, all the other guests formed a circle around them,
clapping hands and shouting in rhythm with the music,
ending with a ringing "Marilyn! Marilyn!" The manager and the waiters held everything in check, and I
didn't notice any fear or apprehension in her demeanor.
She enjoyed it. Antoine was a good dancer, and so was
she; it was a beautiful sight. Now she had also con-
quered the diplomatic corps—and the French one to
boot. We ordered champagne. She got anything she
wanted and more, so when the bandleader came over to

our table and asked her if she would sing "Do It Again," she said:

"Yeah! This is my last evening. Tomorrow I have to work."

She got up on the bandstand, took the microphone, and sang—first "Do It Again" and after that "Diamonds Are a Girl's Best Friend." Her voice was small, but the amplifying system took care of that, and anything she lacked in professional know-how and strength of voice was managed by the doll-like vocal velvet and huskiness reduced to a whisper. It was a thundering success. She was back, she had stopped running, and tomorrow she would arrive back in Hollywood.

In an interview in the August 3, 1962, issue of *Life* magazine, published two days before she died, she said: "You're always running into people's unconscious."

She also ran into her own unconscious.

With the bandage of the spotlights over her eyes.

38th Day

We sat at different ends of the plane. When it landed in Los Angeles, I waited until I had seen her go across the landing strip into the terminal. She was going up to Beverly Hills, and we had agreed that I would send her a message telling her which hotel I had checked into. She would call me when she could.

When dreams come to you, you should surrender to them. I knew this. But you have to say good-bye to them when they leave you—provided you don't go to pieces. I knew I ought to go back to New York, but I wanted to see her once more. It was sentimental, and it would only make things worse. I repeated to myself: Live for a love while it lasts, and try to understand that there are few things in the world more futile than destroying yourself for it when it is no more. But there are moments when even the most bitter experience doesn't suffice.

I took our synopsis out of my suitcase but didn't have the strength to read it again and threw it back in. That, at least, could be overcome.

Evening came. She didn't call.

Before I fell asleep late in the night, I took the synopsis out again and scribbled over the last page: "When you meet beauty, you meet two kinds of truth: that of the body and that of the moment. In my life, still short in years but long in events, I've learned that I must hold on to this moment of truth, cling to it, because only in that way will I experience the wonder of beginning, which is what people call happiness, because I know that one day it will pass. Don't forget that; never forget that."

39th Day

I decided to wait one more day, and that evening she called, out of breath, in a voice so low that it sounded as if she were afraid that someone would overhear. She asked if I could get a car and meet her in an hour at a street corner a short distance north of her hotel.

It was dark when she came, running along the sidewalk from the hotel. She was panting, quickly got into the car beside me, and said:

"If you drive north, out to the Pacific Coast Highway, I know a place."

At first there were cars all around us, but they gradually disappeared, and we drove alone by the tall, dark pine trees which swayed gently in the breeze from the ocean, until we reached a place on the Santa Monica coast where she pointed and said we could park.

I put my arm around her shoulder, and we walked close together down over the sand to the beach, where we sat down.

"Shall we go in?" she asked. "But not too far out. Remember."

We undressed and swam out, but not past where we were able to feel the bottom, then turned around, and lay down in the sand while the water dripped over our bodies. The lights from up on the highway bleached the darkness and made it transparent, and it made her skin shine. We were silent for a long time. Finally I asked:

"When we met in New York—tell me, was there anything you wanted revenge for?"

It took her a long time to reply.

"Yes. But that wasn't the only thing."

Shortly after:

"When we met and you had just come from Africa, was there anything *you* wanted to get revenge for?"

"Yes."

"But that wasn't the only thing either?"

"No, and you know it."

"Yes, but I had to ask. We've been good together. You've been sweet to me."

"But now you have to leave me?"

"Yes, that's how it is. But maybe . . ."

"Maybe. No more maybe."

We lay still, hand in hand, listening to the ocean that stroked the sandy beach with the rhythm of a pulse. Up on the highway cars streaked by once in a while, but their lights couldn't reach us.

"Sometimes," she said, "I dream that I'm buried in sand and that I'm lying and waiting for someone to come and dig me out. I can't do it myself."

Later, when the warm wind from the ocean had dried us, we got up. We dressed and walked up to the car and drove back toward Los Angeles. A short way from her hotel I stopped. We kissed. Her face was very pale. It was the last time I saw her.

40th Day

The next evening I flew back to New York. The plane took off as the sun was setting, the darkness issuing forth rapidly from the American continent. We flew in a circle around Los Angeles and then turned eastward. Down there was the city, Hollywood, Beverly Hills. Like colored fountain water, the green and blue neon signs of movie houses and film studios threw out their garish glow up over the illuminated labyrinth of streets.

It is reported that after the shooting of The Misfits Marilyn told everybody working on the film: "Remember now, cheers, no tears!"

Flying away was like taking a deep breath between love and transience, like a desperate attempt to find harmony between the dream and the earth while looking down on the world I was leaving and which was leaving me. I can understand if people blame me for having written about her. One might say: Reality should live only in the silence of memory. But there are so few people in this world who are brave. She was. It is such a rare *quality that when it is finally encountered, it should not be forgotten.*

There are so many who have wished something for you. I, too, have a wish: If you're ever resurrected, in another being but with the same soul, I wish life would make good again the evil it did you.

Cheers, no tears!

Good-bye, Marilyn!